Carving the Western Path

By River, Rail, and Road Through Central and Northern B.C.

R.G. Harvey

Heritage House

Copyright © 1999 R.G. Harvey

CANADIAN CATALOGUING IN PUBLICATION DATA
Canadian Cataloguing in Publication Data

Harvey, R. G. (Robert Gourlay), 1922-
Carving the western path: by river, rail, and road through central and
northern B.C.

Includes bibliographical references and index.
ISBN 1-895811-74-0

1. Railroads—British Columbia—History.
2. Roads—British Columbia—History.
3. Steam-navigation—British Columbia—History.
4. Paddle steamers—British Columbia—History.
5. Transportation and state—British Columbia—History.
I. Title.

HE215.Z7B714 1999   388'.09711   C99-910162-5

First edition 1999

Heritage House wishes to acknowledge the support of Heritage Canada through
the Book Publishing Industry Development Program, the British Columbia
Arts Council, the Canada Council for the Arts, and the British Columbia
Archives and Records Services (BCARS).

Cover and book design: Darlene Nickull
Editor: Audrey McClellan

HERITAGE HOUSE PUBLISHING COMPANY LTD.
Unit #8 - 17921 55th Ave., Surrey, B.C. V3S 6C4

Printed in Canada

Dedication

This book is dedicated to the two employees of
the Ministry of Transportation and Highways,
A.E. Evenchick and A.G. Munro, who lost their
lives, while serving the people of British Columbia,
in an avalanche in the mountains above the Bell-
Irving River on January 7, 1999.

Those who protect us from the snow
are subject to its hazards. Brave men.

Acknowledgements

The author acknowledges the assistance of the staff of the B.C.
Archives and Records Service and their facilities and, once again,
the help he received from Rodger Touchie, Audrey McClellan,
and Darlene Nickull of Heritage House.

Contents

Maps

Tables

The Asides

Introduction

This narrative history of transportation in British Columbia follows on from the story in the first volume of *Carving the Western Path*, which covered the southern third of the province. This book looks at the development of overland and over-water transportation in central and northern B.C., the remaining two thirds of the province.

In the south the struggle between road and rail was much more defined. They fought not only for the right to use mountain passes, which were few and far between, but also for domination in the moving of goods and people. The first transcontinental railway in Canada, the Canadian Pacific, made no bones about its desire to be pre-eminent in this function, the politics and financial difficulties of its evolution bringing with them a steadfast conviction that such was its right. And many people in Canada, and in British Columbia, believed this too—at least at the beginning, until the problems of a monopoly came into view.

This was why the railway got away with the wanton destruction of the wonderful pioneer road that the colony built through the lower canyons of the Fraser and Thompson rivers with the help of the Royal Engineers, and why it was so successful later on in denying a direct route across the Selkirk Mountains to the road builders. The roundabout route for the first road from Revelstoke to Golden, resulting from the railroaders' initial possession of Rogers Pass, choked off viable long-distance trucking in B.C. until the end of World War II.

Another struggle for ascendancy in crossing the southern mountains came to light along the southern border of the province, where an offshoot of the Canadian Pacific Railway named the Kettle Valley Railway locked horns with an American railway, the Great Northern. In the fuss and fury of that struggle, the roadbuilding program again suffered delays. Parallel to this was the rise and fall of a superb system of lake and river transportation, wonderful within itself, but often manipulated by the railways, and at times detrimental to roads.

A look at the transportation history of the northern two thirds of the province shows that the struggle between modes of movement there was much less obvious, but at times equally dedicated. When the Grand Trunk Pacific Railway built its line from Yellowhead Pass to the Pacific (now the Canadian National Railway's line from Red Pass to Prince Rupert) there were no roads for it to destroy, but it did its best to thwart the building of them, particularly a highway from Prince Rupert to Terrace.

There is no struggle with American railroads in this book—in fact the American influence in transportation, in this case involving roads, was totally benevolent in central and northern British Columbia, even if it took a war to bring it. The United States paid half the cost of the road from Prince Rupert to Terrace, and that country also built a fine highway to Alaska, which ran through the northeast corner of the province, at no cost to Canadians. The sternwheelers bloomed and then wilted, mostly supplementing roads and trails, and again feeling the wrath of the railways for daring to compete. And all of this was overlaid by the search for gold, particularly the finding of it in the Klondike.

The Klondike was in Canada, but the overwhelmingly popular ocean gateway to it was the Alaskan port of Skagway, and it was a British Columbian, William Moore, who first developed Skagway and built the first dock. He also discovered White Pass, which became the avenue to join Skagway to the Yukon by a railroad, one that was built by a Canadian, Michael Haney. Captain Moore—steamboat navigator, winter trail packer, boatbuilder, roadbuilder, and prospector—was an amazing man, and he had the foresight, years before the big find on the Klondike, to anticipate that it was coming. His energy and enterprise run through both volumes of *Carving the Western Path* like a vein of strong blood, as does that of Haney (railway builder), Gus Wright (roadbuilder), John Irving (shipping magnate), and Edgar Dewdney (trail builder): these men built history all over B.C.

Then of course there was that extraordinary pair, the railway contractors then owners, William Mackenzie and Donald Mann (both later knighted). They promoted the building of more and more iron tracks throughout the wilderness all across Canada, dealing with, and mesmerizing, the highest level of politician—premier or prime minister. In my previous writing I described how they brought their Canadian Northern Railway into B.C., resulting in the province gaining a second transprovincial railway, a railway that it did not really need (and in this book it gets another). Here they are no less energetic and persuasive, but in this book their rail lines are more promotional and less real.

Dominating it all, more than the need to prevail or promote or to compete for routes between the different types of carrier, was the harshness of the terrain and climate in the centre and north of the province. Fortunately that brought out the best in the outstanding men and women who lived and worked there. It is all told in the story to follow, and to place you rightly for it, please bear with a little geographic instruction.

Soda Creek, B.C., was, for most of its life, a small, nondescript settlement beside a rather uninteresting stretch of the Fraser River, but in the mid-nineteenth century it had its moment of fame. It was the starting point of navigation on the upper Fraser River. Upstream of Soda Creek the river offered itself as a difficult but not impossible avenue of transportation, one that was extended in the years to come as far as Tete Jaune Cache, a small fur trading post over 400 miles upstream. Initially, however, it was only the first 56 miles upriver that were of concern. They led travellers to

Quesnelmouth, also beside the Fraser and the take-off point of a trail to Barkerville, where Billy Barker had recently found gold in great quantity and where everyone wanted to go in these days.

In 1862, when our story begins, Gustavus Blin Wright and J.C. Galbraith had completed their section of the legendary Cariboo Road from Clinton north to Soda Creek. Wright decided to build a sternwheeler at Soda Creek to convey the road users upriver to Quesnelmouth (later shortened to Quesnel), thus providing a much more comfortable way to travel than by Indian trail or canoe. While a road went in alongside the river within a few years, Wright's SS *Enterprise* did stalwart service for nine crucial years until it was taken away to an adventure to be described later in this book.

In 1862 the Colony of British Columbia was four years old. Its governor, James Douglas, previously chief factor of the Hudson's Bay Company, had initiated the construction of the Cariboo Road to the Interior in 1860. By the end of 1862 this road ran from Yale, the head of navigation on the lower Fraser River, through the Fraser's main canyon, and then up the Thompson River valley to the Cariboo, the lower part of the central interior plateau of British Columbia that lay between the coastal mountains and the Rockies.[1]

This area and the land north of it, made up mostly of rolling hills and some low mountains, had previously been the domain of the North West Company and then the Hudson's Bay Company, which knew it as New Caledonia and a lucrative fur-bearing district.[2] The northern part of the plateau was later called the Lake District due to the number of lakes that it contained, lakes that the fur traders used as their method of travel.

To the north and west, Native tribes on the coast first met what came to be known as the whitecomers (mostly Americans) when they arrived by sail and traded for a transient harvest of sea otter pelts. As the nineteenth century commenced, a sparse population of resident outsiders, who did not depart upon the tide, very slowly grew in numbers along the ocean's edge. They were sustained by the Royal Navy and by the missionaries brought out from England. The fur traders of New Caledonia co-existed well with both the men of God and their flock, and they soon established their ocean outlet at Fort Simpson (later changed to Port Simpson), a few miles up the coast from the later-arriving city of Prince Rupert.

Carrying on from these beginnings, the history of the area has been one of booms and busts, short-lived schemes and dreams, and transient populations. The Barkerville gold discoveries led to the building of the usual shantytowns and the transportation routes (road and river) to serve them, but did little else. Some of the most remarkable twists of transportation history took place in the northeast corner of this Pacific province beyond the Rocky Mountains.

Surprisingly, it was something quite different that started things off in the huge area north and west of Barkerville: a proposal by some Americans to build a communication link with Europe by stringing a telegraph line across B.C. and on to Alaska and Russia. This project was commenced in 1865 and was abruptly terminated in 1867, halfway across the colony, when the trans-Atlantic cable was successfully laid. The telegraph project's contribution to the future development of the colony was a gold find, the result of wintertime prospecting by the telegraph workers on the Omineca River, some 250 miles north of Quesnel. The Omineca gold rush started in 1869 and did not outlast the 1870s, but Manson Creek, at the end of the government trail, was one of its centres that stayed on the map. The rush also opened up a small settlement, soon to be called Hazelton, at the head of navigation on the Skeena River at the other end of the Omineca Trail, and this development brought sternwheelers to that river, operating mostly out of Port Essington. In due course it also led to the building of a railway line that stretched many hundreds of miles across B.C. from Tete Jaune Cache to the mouth of the Skeena, and that railway built Prince Rupert.

But we are getting ahead of our story, which also contains tales of river routes on the far side of the Rocky Mountains and of the building of roads in the northeastern corner of the province, including one to Alaska, events extending well into this century. It goes on to tell of the extension of the sternwheeler world farther north, of the building of trails to serve them at the end of the last century, and of railways, complete and incomplete, to bring in those rushing north to the greatest gold find of them all on the Klondike River.

This is a region of great distances and harsh climate, and at the start of the colonial period the adventurous overland traveller was met by very rough trails (if they existed at all), dangerous river routes, dark canyons, and mountain crossings with avalanches and rockslides to overcome along the way.

The men who brought transportation to this region showed spirit and stamina to a degree seldom equalled anywhere, at any time in history, and both qualities were needed. This is their story.

As with its companion volume, this book comes well illustrated by photographs and maps, and with numerous anecdotes, the latter often drawn from the author's personal experiences in the areas covered.

R.G. Harvey
Victoria, B.C.

Customary to the times when these events occurred, distances and other measures are given in miles and feet rather than in metric measure.
All maps are the work of the author.

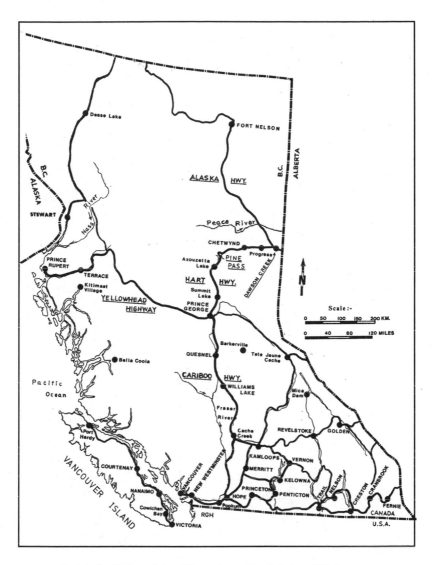

British Columbia Showing the Major Highways

In transportation, the old ways sometimes died slowly. Even half a century after the riverboats of the Skeena first reached Hazelton, pack trains of the legendary Jean Caux (better known as Cataline) made their way overland to the central interior.

Section One

Central British Columbia
from Tete Jaune Cache
to the Pacific Coast

Chapter 1

The Upper Fraser River and the Nechako Valley

Men of the rivers and men of the tracks struggle for supremacy and a single telegraph wire points the way west for rail and road

Two events dominated the provision of overland transportation in central and northwestern British Columbia in its colonial days. One was the discovery of gold on the Omineca River tributaries, which took place in 1869, reached its peak of activity two years later, and then declined. It led to the rapid development of Hazelton, at the head of navigable waters on the Skeena, as a transfer point from river to trail.

The second was a really extraordinary happening that took place just before the Omineca gold rush, between the years 1865 and 1867. It was the survey for, and the partial construction of, an overland telegraph line in British Columbia, conducted by a group of Americans organized as the Collins Overland Telegraph

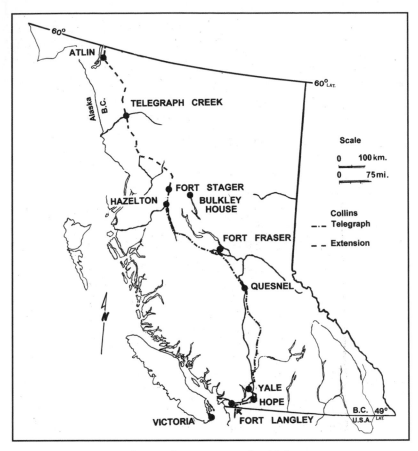

Telegraph Lines to the Yukon

Company, a subsidiary of Western Union. This endeavour was part of a plan to link Europe and America by the recently invented electric telegraph, and true to pioneer enterprise in North America in the nineteenth century, two groups at once engaged in fierce competition.[1]

The Collins Company proposed an overland line from San Francisco through British Columbia, Yukon Territory, and Alaska to Bering Strait, where it would go under water, with the Russians taking over on the other side (see the map "Telegraph Lines to the Yukon"). The second group proposed to go under the Atlantic Ocean. When the first attempt at a trans-Atlantic cable was made in 1857, the cable broke and ended up in pieces on the bottom, quite useless. Two more attempts were made in 1858. One failed and the second succeeded—for one month only. Then the trans-Atlantic line ceased transmitting. Critics claimed the difficulties were insurmountable, and, at least for the time being, this spurred on the Collins people, but they backed the wrong horse.[2]

When the American telegraph workers arrived in the colony of British Columbia in 1865, they were full of optimism. They arrived on the Fraser near Fort Langley and followed the river to Yale, took the Cariboo Road to Quesnel, and then struck out across trackless country to Hazelton. Their reconnaissance and trailblazing in the colony beyond Hazelton ultimately reached as far north as Atlin. Their operations in the colony beyond Hazelton, mostly reconnaissance and trailblazing, ultimately reached as far north as Atlin.

This exploratory survey stretching from south to north in the top half of British Columbia set the pattern for future communication links in the area and proved to be of inestimable value to the province in the years to come.

By 1867 they had strung a landline from the U.S. border at Blaine, Washington, to a point they named Fort Stager about 40 miles north of Hazelton. In addition to building their trail and erecting posts and wire (often using standing trees), they also constructed cabins every 25 miles from Quesnel onwards. They staked out a route by way of Stuart Lake to the head of Takla Lake, where they built Bulkley House, a wintering place for the crew.

The telegraph exploration and construction was under the overall direction of Colonel Charles S. Bulkley, and the field work was led by Captain Edmund Conway, an achiever if there ever was one. The captain wrote to his superior on February 19, 1867:

> We constructed the Telegraph road and line to latitude 55.42 N, and longitude 128.15 W. The distance from Quesnel by the road, is computed at 440 miles, and by the wire 378 miles. There are fifteen stations built, a log

house with chimney, door and windows, 25 miles apart. We built bridges over all small streams, that were not fordable, corduroyed swamps. All hillsides too steep for animals to travel over, were graded, from 3 to 5 feet wide. The average width of clearing the wood for the wire, is, in standing timber, 20 feet: and in fallen timber, 12 feet. All underbrush and small timber is cleared to the ground, thus leaving the road fit for horses, travelling at the rate of, from 30 to 50 miles per day. Double wires are stretched across all rivers. Number of poles put up 9246. Boats are built for crossing the Bulkley and Westroad Rivers.[2]

The above illustrates Captain Conway's efficiency and attention to detail. Following a change of plans—which they said was due to a lack of soil cover in which to found their poles, but which was more likely the result of the man in charge finding what he thought was a better way—Conway dropped the Stuart-Takla Lake route and instead ran a line from Fraser Lake along Burns Lake and Decker Lake to the Bulkley River, and by that valley to Hazelton. The people of B.C. owe him greatly for that route, as it is almost the exact location of the present highway and of the railway from Prince George through Smithers to Hazelton. The early development of the more southerly corridor removed any temptation the railwaymen might have had to follow Stuart and Babine lakes and build alongside them, which would have set a settlement pattern much more difficult to serve with roads later on. From Hazelton the telegraph crew's way led north and west to Telegraph Creek, a choice of great importance to the future development of roads in this area. The men built trail ahead, reaching as far as the Stikine River at Telegraph Creek. This was a bonus to the colony, as the telegraph was never finished. The underwater cable turned out to be entirely feasible, as its builders proved by laying another one successfully in July 1867. Word of this success reached the north late that year, and the unfinished overland alternative was immediately abandoned.[3]

Franklin Leonard Pope sketched Bulkley House (bottom) while in the Collins Telegraph camp in 1867. He also sketched the telegraph workers' whiling away the long B.C. winter evenings (top). The inclusion of snowshoes is of interest. As late as 1873 the Royal Navy, which was conducting expeditions to the Arctic in search of Sir John Franklin, refused their use as impracticable. They were an invention of the North American native population, here in use by the American telegraph crew.

It is unfortunate that Conway's name is not perpetuated locally. His superior is immortalized in the naming of a major river, a foreman was equally honoured by Decker Lake, and another landmark, Burns Lake, was misnamed after the leading surveyor, a man by the name of Michael Byrne, but Conway got nothing.[4] Much of the telegraph line was abandoned when the project died, except for the section as far as Quesnel, which was extended to Barkerville and promptly put into operation. The line from Quesnel westwards and the surplus wire stores, cabins, etc., were simply left to rot. The Native people at Hazelton, which was then known as Skeena Forks, cleverly used the surplus wire to build a suspension bridge across a ravine containing the Bulkley River at Hagwilget. It lasted for many years, to the amazement of all engineers who saw it. The wire was the diameter of a soda straw.

The telegraph surveyors' original route to Bulkley House (a place shown on the map "Lake Country") was followed in part many years later by a railway in this area. Premier W.A.C. Bennett, who wished to put the area west and north of the Skeena to use, came up with a proposal that foundered just as absolutely as many others in the area. He built a railway parallel to the Grand Trunk Pacific Railway and about 40 miles north of it, and he reached some distance past Bulkley House before the lack of anything there and of anything reasonably easy to develop became obvious. Reason prevailed and his dream was abandoned, and some of the results of it were turned into a resource road.

Bennett's route followed the traditional path of the fur traders in New Caledonia. It went from Summit Lake, just north of Prince George, via Stuart Lake and Takla Lake to Bulkley House, then north and west to the Stikine country. The Hudson's Bay men went by the same route to Takla Lake, except they travelled by boat and canoe on Stuart Lake, Babine Lake, Takla Lake, and the rivers and lakes in between. It was an efficient means of getting around a country dotted with lakes that stretched from Babine Village to Fort St. James, the administrative centre of the Hudson's Bay Company in that area. In the late 1880s the HBC made a rather tentative decision to abandon the Fraser River and make Port Simpson its ocean shipping point and supply centre for New Caledonia. The route was by boat for the length of Stuart Lake, over an 11-mile portage to Babine Lake, down its 100-mile length to Babine Village, then by the trail to Hazelton and down the Skeena to a portage to Wark Inlet and Port Simpson (see maps "Lake Country" and "Rivers and a Railroad"). It never really worked out, and the company soon abandoned the idea, although its sternwheelers continued to ply the Skeena for many years. In

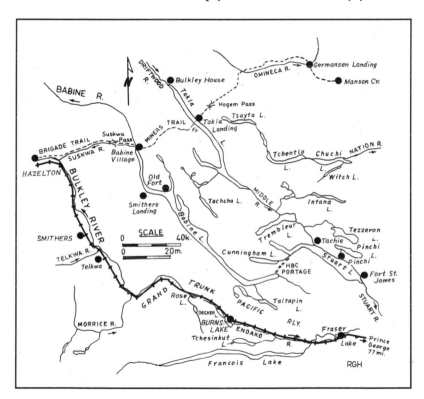

Lake Country

The routes across central British Columbia, from the top, are—
The trail to Omineca gold. Hazelton to Manson Creek.
The fur traders route. Babine Lake to Stuart Lake.
The Grand Trunk Pacific Railway.
(Roads and highways omitted.)

The bridge over Hagwilget Canyon on the Bulkley River, which was built by the Indians with surplus wire from the Collins Overland Telegraph. It replaced one that was built with cedar poles tied with cedar bark. (Also see close up of this bridge on back cover.)

1911 the HBC was still operating a sailing schooner on Stuart and Babine lakes, hauling it on a wagon over the twelve-mile-long portage road between them.[5]

That the Collins Telegraph men went into this area at all meant that they must have had the blessing of the HBC, probably through Governor Seymour, who no doubt requested the Chief Factor at Fort St. James, Peter Skene Ogden, to give them every assistance. Considering the type of man Ogden was, they would have got nowhere without his co-operation, which ensured that they would have no fur trader nor tribal opposition. Ogden captained six fur-trading trips up the Snake River from the Columbia as far as Utah and California for the HBC between 1818 and 1824. Ogden, Utah, was named after him. He took on all comers, including American mountain men, and was reported to be very hard on his crew. In 1834 he had journeyed to the Stikine in an attempt to found Fort Stikine, but was rebuffed by the Russians (that fort finally came into being in 1839). No doubt he had mellowed by

This photograph shows a pack train assembling at Hazelton bound for Babine Lake. The man who is hatless, in the foreground, is Jean Jacques Caux, known as Cataline, "the best packer in B.C., if not in North America." He packed on the Cariboo Road when it first opened, then from Quesnel to Barkerville before there was a road, and then from Hazelton to Manson Creek, and it is said he never once failed to deliver. Alex Lord, pioneer school inspector, met him in the Omineca Hotel in Hazelton in 1916, drinking rum, which he first poured into his shoulder-length iron-grey hair as was his custom. A year later the hotel burned down. Cataline first escaped; then he went back to his room for a treasured pair of boots, and the roof fell on him. It was a fitting end.

the time he was chief factor in New Caledonia in 1867 (he was then 71 and was known as Whitetop because of his shock of white hair), but he was still a hard man. He could teach the telegraph men a lot about that wilderness.

In the course of their reconnaissance the Collins men acquired a sternwheeler with which to scout out all the major waterways running in from the Pacific coast to the unmapped area they would have to go through. Unfortunately the vessel, built for them in Seattle and named the *Mumford*, was designed in the eastern States, and the designers underestimated the force of the current in B.C.'s wild rivers, particularly the Skeena, which had the strongest flow of them all. The *Mumford* only got part way up to Hazelton, but their supplies were carried forward, with the help of the local Native people, to what became a key location for the change from river to trail.[6]

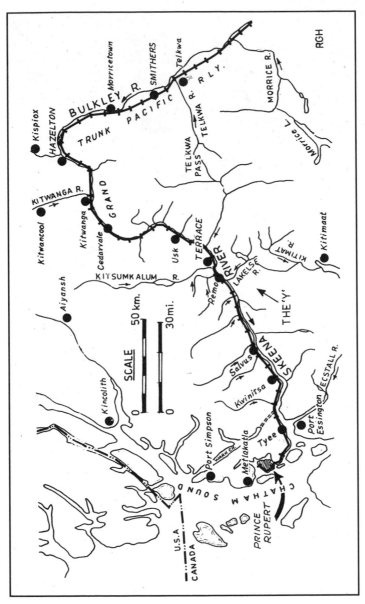

The long inlet to the east of Port Simpson is Wark Channel (sometimes Work Channel). The double dashed line from the outlet of the Khyex River (which is the first stream shown west of Kwinitsa) to Wark Channel is the old HBC portage. Tributary rivers unnamed are, from Kwinitsa easterly: Kasiks, Exchamsiks, Exstew, and Shames; and from Terrace easterly: Copper, Kleanza, Legate and Little Oliver.

No one of good judgment starts off into the wilderness without using all means of access to civilization along the way, and civilization's doorstep in this part of the world at that time was the Pacific Ocean. The telegraph crews fully intended to use the Skeena River, the Stikine, and the Nass to service their line. This was probably another reason for the route change away from Bulkley House; had they gone by way of Takla Lake as they originally intended, they would have missed both the Skeena and the Nass as avenues to the ocean.

Two final thoughts on the Collins Overland Telegraph Company's expedition into the colony of British Columbia and the northern wilderness adjoining it in 1866: First, when the force of about 150 men wintered at Bulkley House, they did not sit on their hands; they prospected for gold and some of them found colour in the headwaters of the Omineca. When the project collapsed, some of these men returned to the river and soon the word was out and the rush was on.[7] The Omineca excitement, and the Collins operation that started it, both contributed greatly to the early development of the northwestern quarter of British Columbia, even though neither lasted very long.

The second thought is of more international significance. How much did the movement of these former Americans through what was soon to become the Alaska panhandle serve to firm up the hand of American Secretary of State William Seward when he signed the agreement to purchase Alaska from Russia in 1867? This is a good question for British Columbians to mull over as they view their current salmon-fishing problems.

The dominion government restarted work on the Collins line in 1898 and extended it from Hazelton to Telegraph Creek and on to Atlin by 1902 to establish communication with Dawson City during the Klondike gold rush. The government also built a similar line and trail from Hazelton to Port Simpson.[8] When the CPR telegraph went into operation in 1886 it replaced the section from New Westminster to Yale and on to Spences Bridge, and the Grand Trunk Pacific Railway took over the line from Vanderhoof to Hazelton when it came on the scene.

In the meantime, road, river, and rail transportation was being developed in this north-central part of the province. Native peoples had travelled through the area for centuries, and the HBC had been there from near the beginning of the 1800s, travelling by canoe and on foot. In the 1860s the Cariboo Road arrived from the south, built by G. B. Wright and J. C. Galbraith on contract. As soon as he reached open water on the Fraser at Soda Creek, Wright built a sternwheeler that he named the *Enterprise*. The *Enterprise* was a fine boat and it served the route from Soda Creek to Quesnel steadfastly from 1863 to 1871, continuing to offer comfortable and dust-free transport after Wright's road went in alongside it.

The year 1871 was when the gold rush to the Omineca got under way, first thought of as another Barkerville, though quickly proven otherwise. Edgar Dewdney, the foremost surveyor and trail builder in the colony, mapped out a direct route to the Omineca gold findings, following the telegraph trail to Fraser Lake and then running alongside Stuart and Takla lakes to Manson Creek. As usually happened, boat service was put in on the intervening lakes, and in due course a road was built stretching the 170 miles from Fort St. James to Manson Creek. Another 25 miles were added to take it to Germansen Landing. Maintaining this 200 miles of road, which was mainly used by northern prospectors, was a severe burden on the Department of Public Works for many years, despite intermittent funding from the Mines Branch. It was a horror in the spring, when a wheel placed too close to the edge of the road would disappear in mud that had the texture of stucco-mix. The author had personal and disastrous experience of this when a wrong move while attempting to pass a bogged-down logging truck led to the disappearance of two wheels. A very difficult digging and jacking-up operation was carried out whilst being eaten alive by blackflies.

Getting back to the Omineca rush of the 1870s, in the first surge of excitement Gus Wright succumbed to the scent of gold, as everyone did in those years. Without hesitation he accompanied

The main street of Hazelton (c. 1908). The Omineca Hotel is at the centre right. Hazelton is situated by a steelhead trout river, the Bulkley, with the rugged peaks of the Babine Range of the Skeena Mountains behind.

the *Enterprise* in June of that year on what was to be its last trip. Fully laden with freight and passengers, it headed for an area that was 200 miles as the crow flies north and west of Quesnel. The only way to get there was via rivers and lakes that were treacherous and uncharted (except by rough Hudson's Bay Company mapping), quite unknown to the boat's navigators, and all within the primeval wilderness.[9]

Its first test was the Cottonwood Canyon on the Fraser, which it struggled through to Fort George (the original name of Prince George). Then it took on the fast-flowing Nechako River to the Stuart River, and continued up its winding course to Stuart Lake. Finally it traced the Tachie River to Trembleur Lake, and the Middle River to Takla Lake. Today visitors to the area, noting the shallows, log jams, and rapids on the Tachie and the Middle rivers, shake their heads in wonderment at this trip.

The *Enterprise* did not get to the Omineca, because that river was outside the watershed of the Fraser, but it did get to Takla Landing on Takla Lake, which was only about 50 miles by trail

The Enterprise *at Soda Creek in 1868. In 1863, the* Enterprise *was built at a point near Alexandria, a few miles upstream from Soda Creek. The boat was 110 feet in length and 20 feet in beam, and its engine, shaft, and boiler plate were packed in on mules over the Harrison-Lillooet Trail. The* Enterprise *gave excellent service on the 60-mile trip to Quesnel, offering two round-trips per week for eight years and connecting with Frank Barnard's stagecoach operation, carrying passengers, mail, and express from Soda Creek to Yale, which got underway on May 1, 1864, and lasted for a full 50 years until it was replaced by the automobile.*

The Enterprise *was under the command of Captain Thomas Wright, whose kinship to the owner is unclear. In 1871 it was taken off the run and sent north to serve the Omineca gold rush, travelling more than 200 miles north and west of Quesnel over uncharted and untravelled waterways to the upper end of Takla Lake. On its way back it started to come apart on Trembleur Lake and was beached. The remains of the old vessel were eventually consumed by fire. Its ironwork is still there.*

from the Omineca. The profit from the fares and from the sale of the supplies it carried more than paid for replacing the boat. This was a good thing because the *Enterprise* never made it back to Quesnel. On its return the old vessel came apart in Trembleur Lake and was beached there. A sternwheeler's life was never long.[10]

The *Victoria*, launched in 1869 by Robert McLeese, Soda Creek merchant and Member of the Provincial Parliament (as MLAs were called then), replaced the *Enterprise* on the Cariboo service. It plied the Fraser from Soda Creek to Quesnel until 1886, when it too died of old age and was hauled out at Fort Alexandria. Nothing moved on the river for ten years until the *Charlotte*

These nineteenth-century photos show Fort St. James at the southeast end of Stuart Lake. Today the community is the northern terminus of the paved section of Highway 27 from Vanderhoof.

appeared and carried on by itself up until 1909.[11] By that time excitement caused by the expectation of the Pacific Great Eastern Railway (PGE) and the construction of the Grand Trunk Pacific Railway (GTP) gripped the area, helped on by Premier Richard McBride. The PGE was not to reach beyond Quesnel for many years (see Chapter 4). Nonetheless it and the GTP, and several others which were forecast, helped George J. Hammond, with the aid of his brother and half a million dollars in advertising, sell no less than 12,000 lots around Fort George, most of which eventually turned out to be worthless. Some even disappeared under a normal spring flood on the Fraser. It was a shameful chapter in B.C.'s history of real estate promotion, but it did launch some sternwheelers, including one called the *Robert C. Hammond* (named after his son).[12]

The first was the *Nechacco*, a small boat with a draft of only thirteen inches, launched in 1909. Following in the wake of the

In 1911, William Weathall photographed this pack train of Indian dogsleds along the Skeena River Trail from Hazelton to Manson Creek.

Enterprise (churned up 38 years before), it too struggled up the Nechako River from Fort George, but instead of travelling the Stuart River to Stuart Lake it continued up the Nechako to the Nautley River, which provides a short connection to Fraser Lake. Once there it served the GTP railbuilders along the lake's twelve-mile length. (This trip is recorded for posterity by two photographs taken of the vessel on the river. These are on file in the B.C. Archives.[13]) The *Nechacco* was skippered on this trip by Captain J.H. Bonser, a fearless mariner from the Skeena who in 1902 had set the speed record for the round trip from Port Essington to Hazelton and back: 47 hours for the 360 miles. With Bonser, the *Nechacco* also made the first trip from Fort George to Tete Jaune Cache up the Fraser. The *Nechacco* was renamed the *Chilco*, probably because they could no longer stand the misspelling, and the *Chilco* blew its steam pipes while challenging the current in the Cottonwood Canyon in 1910. It capsized and disappeared, with the crew barely making their escape.[14]

The Chilco, *formerly the* Nechacco, *one of the sturdy little vessels with stout-hearted skippers that plied difficult rivers.*

More boats were launched in 1910, and that of the most interest and longevity was the *B.X.*, a hardy vessel owned by the stagecoach company of that nickname, formerly the Barnard Express and more lately the B.C. Express Company. It cost an unheard-of $53,000. After its launch in May 1910, the *B.X.* had no difficulty with Cottonwood Canyon and served the route from Soda Creek to Fort George for a number of years, with, however, a rather chequered economic career. Beached late in 1915 by lack of business due to the war and resurrected in May 1918, its second life lasted only sixteen months before it struck a rock in Fort George Canyon and sank.

While the *B.X.* was out of action, three gas launches—the *Circle W*, the *Rounder*, and the *Viper*—filled in on the haul from Quesnel to Fort George. They made the 90-mile trip in about nine hours. There was profit in this as goods that travelled from Edmonton to Fort George by rail and continued by boat to Quesnel were cheaper than those that came from the south.[15]

In 1912, according to Cliff Kopas, a later traveller in the area, "an amazing thing happened to Tete Jaune Cache...it became—

Sideways was the way that the sternwheelers sometimes went through the rough canyon waters when the helmsman was slow to spin the wheel. Left, the Charlotte *is going through Cottonwood Canyon upstream from Quesnel on the Fraser. Sometimes* Charlotte *didn't make it through altogether dry, but it was refloated after the grounding below.*

Old and new spellings differ, and for whatever reason they changed the name of the Nechacco *to the* Chilco *fairly early in its life. It was a short one, as the* Chilco *blew its steam pipes in the Cottonwood Canyon of the Fraser in 1910 and sank, fortunately without loss of life. Here it challenges the Nechako, skimming the rocks with its draft of thirteen inches, on its way to Fraser Lake. The bottom photo shows the* Nechacco's *Captain Bonser, pioneer sternwheeler skipper, the man with the naval cap and the mustache. He has just conveyed a group of settlers to the banks of the Nechako River in 1910. A sternwheeler passenger once said of these early means of travel, "They brought pioneer civilisation to the area," and these hardy souls had just left this semblance of good living to experience much less of it.*

This photo of the Victoria *under construction on the bank of the Fraser River at Quesnel in 1868 shows the primitive facilities they used for ship building in these days—dreadfully vulnerable to ice jam or spring flooding. The engines and boiler came up the Lillooet Trail and Cariboo Road from the Lillooet Lake steamer* Prince of Wales. *These hard-to-obtain parts were regularly interchanged. The secondhand machinery worked very well for eighteen years, after which the* Victoria *was hauled out and the river was left at peace for ten years.*

of all things—a shipbuilding centre." The Grand Trunk Pacific Railway had reached Mile 49 from Yellowhead Pass that year. It shipped two sternwheelers in parts from Prince Rupert to the Cache, and "two ships, 141.7 feet long by 34.8 feet in beam were rebuilt and launched." These were the *Operator* and the *Conveyor*. They immediately went into service between Fort George and Tete Jaune Cache. Their captains were from the Skeena, so no rapids nor canyons would deter them![16]

Scows and rafts were also built to float down the Fraser River from Tete Jaune Cache to the Grand Canyon of the Fraser, dropping off materials along the way. Often they continued on through the canyon to Fort George, at great danger to the men and materials on them. They were then dismantled (if they made it) and hauled back to Tete Jaune Cache by sternwheeler. The total number of men working on the water in 1913 reached 2000, and 50 of them drowned in the river that year, 20 of them in the Grand Canyon.[17]

Launched in 1912, the *B.X.*'s sister ship, the *B.C. Express*, was a much larger vessel capable of carrying 200 passengers. During 1912 and most of 1913 it battled the strong current of the Fraser from Soda Creek not only to Fort George, but also around the bend of the river to Tete Jaune Cache, another 315 miles. Every week it brought $5000 in profits for the owners, largely due to the skill of the navigator, Captain J.E. Bucey. How he negotiated the Grand Canyon of the Fraser, the Giscome Rapids, and the Goat River Rapids repeatedly without one mishap, no one knew, but he did it.[18]

Cliff Kopas travelled through Barkerville in 1933. He talked to the old-timers there, and in his book *Packhorses to the Pacific* he reported that the boat service to Tete Jaune Cache lasted until 1920, but it did not. It ceased in the summer of 1913, at a point about 90 miles upstream of Fort George, when the Grand Trunk

The passengers are workers coming off leave to return to Grand Trunk Pacific Railway construction upstream of Fort George. The vessel, Conveyor, *was brought from the Skeena to help with the construction. It was a sister ship to the* Operator, *the* Omineca, *and the* Distributor.

The name was the only thing small about the B.X., certainly not its longevity of service on the upper Fraser nor its standing in that good company of river craft. Red velvet carpets and steam heat meant luxury in these days, and the conductor stood ready at the gangplank to lead you to it. The B.X. came to a sad end on August 30, 1919 (below). Although salvaged, the boat did not go back into service.

This view of a scow navigating the Grand Canyon of the Fraser in 1913 shows the danger that GTP Railway contractor Foley, Welch and Stewart placed its employees in as they brought materials and equipment cheaply from Tete Jaune Cache down river. It is said that twenty men drowned that season in the canyon.

Pacific Railway strung a steel cable across the Fraser River at the confluence of Dome Creek, the first step in the building of two low-level bridges (the second was at Upper Fraser).

To digress for a moment, Cliff Kopas and his wife Ruth were on a honeymoon trip from Calgary, Alberta, travelling slightly north of west, but quite directly across the Rocky Mountains, the Cariboo Mountains, the interior plateau of British Columbia, and the Coast Mountains, ending up at the Pacific in a small settlement called Bella Coola on North Bentinck Arm of Burke Channel. They settled there and lived happily thereafter. They were accompanied on this trip by several packhorses, which gave his account of the journey its title, and his delightful book describes a wonderful trip, illustrated by excellent photographs and maps.[19] Rediscovering history, Cliff and Ruth visited most of the Rocky Mountain passes used by Native peoples and fur traders, and after choosing Yellowhead Pass they retraced the less-travelled route of some of the gold seekers bound for Barkerville in the 1860s. As

This view of Tete Jaune Cache in 1908 makes it obvious why the railwaymen working here spent their leave elsewhere. Most of the town was later washed into the Fraser River by flood waters.

Seen here in 1912, Tete Jaune Cache was about to become the launch site of two new sternwheelers to assist the railway workers.

these miners did, the Kopases came to Tete Jaune Cache from the east, then went up the Fraser River for about 70 miles to Goat River. Taking the trail of that name, they made their way across the Cariboo Range to Bowron Lake and on to Barkerville and Quesnel. By using that route they saved about 200 miles over the alternative of following the long bend of the Fraser from Tete Jaune Cache to Quesnel (see map of "The Upper Fraser").[20]

The B.C. Express *also carried the opposition—wagons!*

This was a difficult shortcut. Before they took it in 1933 it had been unused for twenty years, since the building of the GTP from Yellowhead to Fort George in 1912 and 1913. The extreme steepness, poor weather (constant rain), and wet and slippery clay of Goat Pass Trail had one tragic effect on the Kopas expedition. The descent from the divide was disastrous for the packhorses, which often slipped to their haunches on the rough ground. The lead horse, his spirit broken, refused to continue when they reached civilization and had to be left with a rancher at Barkerville.[21] We are indebted to Kopas for his description of that historic trail, which cost him a fine animal. The highway builders in the 1960s had similar trouble with that same clay and that same weather when they built a bridge across Goat River.

Kopas obviously was unwilling to face the expense and difficulty of shipping his three packhorses and their loads by train, especially given that there was only one run per week, so he was forced to use the mountain trail. That there was no better road nor trail around the length of the Fraser as a substitute to the railway, nor any rivercraft to offer an alternative to that awful trail when Kopas arrived, is an example of the precedence of the railroad in western Canada. Even though the trail was there first, it was not maintained or modernized, and the railway also ousted the regular sternwheeler service in effect between 1909 and 1913.

In the early 1930s, that area of the province needed a road system with one or more bridge or ferry crossings of the Fraser River. What it had instead was a bankrupt railway barely supported by an unwilling government at the other end of the country. After 1933, when the depression really took hold in the province, the once-proud transcontinental railway across the centre of British Columbia was reduced in status to a branch line of the Canadian National.

At the time of its building, the Grand Trunk was grossly premature to the development of the need for it in central and northwestern B.C. In addition, railways have never solved the immediate transportation needs of a locality very well, especially

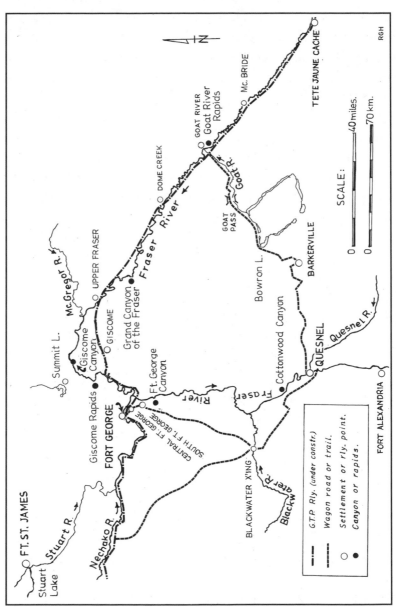

The Upper Fraser, circa 1911

when there are settlements across a river from the track. The result was that the GTP was never economically viable, and its financial position worsened steadily in the Great Depression. When a railway is not breaking even, the regularity and frequency of freight and passenger service drops drastically, which is what happened between Prince George (the name adopted in 1915) and Tete Jaune Cache, and to McBride, the town that became the centre for its area. (McBride never approached the status of Prince George, good railway or bad, because it had to wait 50 years for a road of any kind to Prince George and 40 years for a fully usable road south. It proved that, starting in the second quarter of the twentieth century, any town in B.C. needed good road access in at least two directions to fully expand.)

Add to this the fact that at least one company, the B.C. Express, was ready and willing to maintain another mode of transportation—steamboats—that had proved to be a better means of serving both sides of the valley lower down on the same river, and the decision not to install short lift spans in the railway bridges at Dome Creek and Upper Fraser comes out as a dreadful mistake. This decision and the fate of Cliff Kopas's horse are two black marks on the record sheet of Ottawa's Board of Railway Commissioners, and also on that of the dominion government.

The railway tried to obtain the BRC's approval to block navigable waters. It did not receive this approval but blocked the river anyway, with no repercussions from the federal government. The B.C. Express Company launched a lawsuit that went as far as the Privy Council in London, but it could not prevent the closure of the Fraser to sternwheelers at Dome Creek and Upper Fraser. This is even more difficult to understand in light of the installation of a lift span in the railway bridge at Prince George, though the railway finally took all the steamboats out of service in 1921.[22]

The persistent need for river travel arose because of the lack of a road beside the Fraser River above Prince George, as well as the need for access to each bank of the river. There was a road due east from Prince George to the village of Giscome, but Department

In the name of progress, the Operator *transports a construction engine through the Grand Canyon of the Fraser. The engine would help build a line that eventually led to the sternwheelers' demise. By 1929 only the rotting hulls of two grand derelicts, the* Conveyor *and* Operator, *remained.*

of Public Works crews always had their hands full keeping it open. Every spring it had to be extensively planked due to the action of the frost on the underlying soil, and it usually took all summer to recover from this. This road maintenance problem continued for another 20 miles to Upper Fraser. Beyond this crossing there was no continuous road on either side of the river for over 90 miles to McBride until the highway went through on the south side of the river in the 1970s. It was and still is one of the worst stretches of highway in the province for difficult soil conditions combined with wet and snowy weather.

There is little doubt that the *Enterprise* and the other boats that joined it contributed to settlements appearing in areas without road access alongside the upper Fraser, but it was the GTP railway that strung them out all the way from Prince George to McBride, a situation that took many years to rectify. Both the railway and the sternwheelers brought problems to the road authority to the east of Prince George, but not to the west (see the next chapter).

A problem of a different sort was created when construction crews were based in the vicinity of Tete Jaune Cache. A rivalry arose between the representatives of Kamloops, Salmon Arm, and Golden as to which town would supply them. Kamloops won out and a wagon road was built up the North Thompson valley. This road became the responsibility of the Department of Public Works, which had to maintain it even though for the next 50 years there was not enough settlement at its northern end to justify its existence.[23]

As for travel south of Prince George, although there was no railway, there were some alternatives, both old and new, before and after the war. The B.C. Express Company introduced two Winton 6 automobiles to run between Soda Creek and Ashcroft in 1910, and the fleet had grown to eight by 1913. Each car could carry six passengers and little more than their baggage. For an older alternative, Martin Starret, a young adventurer who grew up in Hope and went fur trading on Babine Lake in 1909, reports that a crew from the Babine Lake fish hatchery headed south in

1911 and travelled by boat to Stuart Lake, by canoe to Quesnel, by the sternwheeler *B.X.* to Soda Creek, and then by horse-drawn stagecoach to Ashcroft.

Twenty-seven years earlier, Newton Chittenden went before them in exactly the same manner from Quesnel to Ashcroft. Chittenden, an American who travelled extensively in B.C. in the early 1880s, travelled on Robert McLeese's *Victoria.*[24]

We leave Prince George in the early 1920s as the town finally realizes that its sternwheelers are gone forever and that having a railway does not mean automatic prosperity—not much of a prelude to the Great Depression. It would be three decades, into the 1950s, before there was a road from Prince George to the Peace River area and railways north and south, and ten years after that before the Department of Public Works finally had the knowledge and resources to overcome the area's poor weather and soil conditions and build fully spring-thaw-resistant paved highways, including one to McBride. Then the boom took off.

The B.C. Express Company, also known as the BX Company, realizing in 1909 that the demise of the horse-drawn stagecoach was fast approaching, moved with the times and courageously introduced the horseless carriage to the Cariboo Road as a business venture. The company's intent was to move passengers quickly between Ashcroft, where the CPR turned east, and Soda Creek. From there they would continue by river to Quesnel and Fort George on the sternwheeler B.X., which the company had under construction that year.

The BX Company sent a man south to choose a suitable vehicle. After the Packard sales agent in Vancouver refused to take him out on a test run because it was raining, the man from the Cariboo went to Seattle, where the Winton 6 agent won the day by driving him around, having a good parts inventory, and promising to send drivers with mechanical knowledge to the Cariboo to break in men from B.C. The company purchased two demonstration models initially, and finally a total of eight Winton Six automobiles followed after the first two proved themselves.

The bodies were painted the same colour as the company's stagecoaches: bright red with yellow wheels. During the life of these chassis the wooden bodies were rebuilt several times by B.C. craftsmen. The cars, as shown above, were right-hand drive; it was not mandatory to drive on the right side of the road in the Interior of B.C. until January 16, 1920. Drivers continued to drive on the left in the Lower Mainland and on Vancouver Island until December 1, 1921.

Pioneer Fort George newspaper editor Russell Walker reported that in 1911 the Duke of Sutherland visited the Fort George area with a large party to look over the area for investment in railways or land. Walker says the Duke rented four Winton Sixes, three for people and one for liquor. This might be the group shown here.

THE PRIZEWINNER

The railways played many dirty tricks on other forms of transportation in British Columbia in order to reduce competition. If awards were given for these tricks, then the Grand Trunk Pacific Railway would easily take first prize for the game it played with the B.C. Express Company in the summer of 1913.

The express company owned the BX and the B.C. Express, and together these two boats were the best on the upper Fraser. Helped greatly by their outstanding fast-water skipper Captain J.E. Bucey, they were clearing $5000 a week in profits that summer on the run from Fort George to Tete Jaune Cache. Then the GTP lowered the boom, literally, and announced that it was placing two low-level bridges across the Fraser River between Fort George and Tete Jaune Cache. To underline this, workers strung a cable at low level over the river at Dome Creek (Mile 141), one of the crossings, and railway contractor Foley, Welch and Stewart immediately threatened physical violence to anyone interfering with it. The second crossing was at Upper Fraser, Mile 183.

This was done despite a ruling by the Board of Railway Commissioners in Ottawa forbidding such action. Neither the BRC, a regulating agency of the Canadian Parliament, nor the dominion government appears to have taken any action against the GTP's defiance of that ruling.

After Captain Bucey was restrained from taking a shotgun to the railwaymen, his company went to court, seeking damages and an injunction to remove the cable. The B.C. Express Company's high-paid lawyer in Vancouver suddenly withdrew just before the case came up, and the case was bungled—strike one. The appeal to the B.C. Supreme Court won approval, but a subsequent appeal by the railway won a Canadian Supreme Court ruling in its favour—strike two. Never giving up, the B.C. Express Company went to the Privy Council in London. There history repeated itself, the company's British counsel suddenly left, and the case collapsed—strike three. Sternwheelers disappeared from the upper Fraser River, and the railway had a clear field from Tete Jaune Cache (Mile 53) to Fort George (Mile 230). It would be 50 years before a highway challenged the train.

The rivermen deserved much better than this from the government in Ottawa, and from Premier McBride, who was to be honoured by the naming of the town that they would never serve.

(The mileages given are the railway's distance from the Alberta boundary and are approximate.)[25]

Chapter 2

Through to the Middle Coast

*A town dies and one is built, and a world war
widens the cliffs of the Skeena Valley to
let a road in beside the railway*

The western portion of the Grand Trunk Railway, which was called the Grand Trunk Pacific, was a courageous dream in British Columbia; it passed through an area about 400 miles in length and 100 miles wide, which in 1903 contained not even one settlement where the non-Native population could support a school district. It was aimed at the centre of a remarkable society on the Pacific coast. This society enjoyed a culture more complex and profound than was ever imagined by the outsiders who had barely scratched its veneer on casual visits during the preceding hundred years, or by the settlers who had not looked below its surface during their 50 years of occupation to that date.

One indication of the scope of this civilization is the fact that of ten separate aboriginal linguistic groups in British Columbia, seven are located on the Pacific coast. These were more than just a collection of differing dialects, and no less than four of them converged in the area where the railway proposed to arrive at salt water after following the Skeena River through the Coast Mountains.

The four groups that the railway would now descend upon were the Tsimshian of the Skeena and Nass valleys, including the Gitksan and the Nisga'a nations; the Haisla, represented by the Kitimaat community; and farther east, near the mountains and

The Native tribes of British Columbia's coast expressed themselves artistically in ways defying description. The upper photograph is of a Haida village on the Queen Charlotte Islands, the lower of a lodge at Bella Coola. Both were taken by Edward Dossetter in 1881. It seemed that the men declined to be photographed, but the women and children obliged.

part of the Athapaska group whose territory spread right across the Interior Plateau, the Babines or Nat'oot'en. Last of all there was the Haida nation, the most developed and the most menacing of them all, located on the Queen Charlotte Islands. The Haidas were much less sedentary and more aggressive than the others, as they showed in their whaling forays to the open Pacific and in their voyaging abroad. They regularly indulged in slave-taking raids, usually preying on the tribes of the lower coast or Vancouver Island.

Slave-taking and the abandonment of it gives an excellent example of how quickly the Pacific coast First Nations adapted to the entry of the Europeans. All of the coast nations took slaves as bounty when they were successful in warfare. Usually they treated them well, sometimes releasing them after faithful and good service, but when the European traders first arrived on the coast about a hundred years before the arrival of the railway, they were particularly distressed by one savage custom of the local chiefs. This was their practice of occasionally and rather casually putting one or more of their slaves to death as a means of gaining status, either when they were being visited by other chiefs, or at a funeral or potlatch. The Hudson's Bay men refused to recognize or deal with any chiefs who did this, and the practice disappeared.

Most of the time these different nations traded with each other quite peacefully. Each sought from the other the bounty of nature particular to the other's region, or artifacts of the other's craftsmanship, which were often of the highest quality. The northwest coast people built large and magnificent dugout canoes, post-and-beam cedar lodges, cedar-planked houses, riverwide fish traps of amazing complexity, and even cedar boxes that could store water, and they worshipped and conserved their salmon resource. One perceptive HBC man described it as a cedar and salmon civilization, and it was. The basic social unit was the village community or sometimes simply a family or clan.[1]

This society on the west coast of British Columbia had met the European traders from overseas on remarkably level ground.

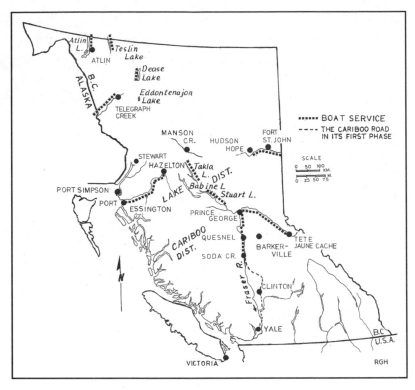

Lake and River Routes of Central and Northern B.C.

There was the infrequent taking of a ship on a lonely coast and the massacre of the crew, but this was almost always when the seaborne intruders were either unwatchful or behaved less than reasonably. Very occasionally there had been attacks on remote HBC posts or expeditions, but these traumatic events were widely separated in time and space, and they had more or less come to an end by the end of the century, as had most of the intertribal warfare and slave-taking raids.

The sum and substance of this is that when the eastern railway tycoons and the politicians who supported them decided to bring a railway to an aboriginal population that had neither the slightest interest in it nor use for it and were in no way consulted about it, that population had generally reached a balance with those who had come by sea. This equilibrium was sustained primarily by the

Christian missionary establishment that had sprung up in the area, assisted by the Royal Navy and by the Hudson's Bay Company with its enlightened aboriginal policies. This equilibrium was very fortunate for all of the parties concerned, as it meant there was no resistance to the railway-builders. It was not something the railway barons had earned. The invasion of the white man had been gradual, usually peaceful, and in most cases satisfactory to both sides. The railway was simply a needless aberration. To the people of the raven, who had been there for millennia, it was a strange and unknown visitation, and one that did not depart upon the tide.

This was not a concern to Prime Minister Sir Wilfrid Laurier, the Liberal who was elected to head the dominion government in 1896 and who held office until 1911. In 1903 he informed the nation that his government was backing a second cross-country railway to the Pacific coast. As was the case in B.C. some years later when Richard McBride announced his support for the Canadian Northern Railway, ministerial departure immediately followed—Laurier's minister of railways resigned. The railway went ahead, anyway, as that was the way to political happiness in these days, or at least that was what they thought. (The minister who resigned was A.G. Blair, who was reported to be very close to William Mackenzie and Donald Mann, railway promoters we will meet in Chapter 4.)[2]

The new railway went by the name of the Grand Trunk Pacific, and it was to enter B.C. by way of Yellowhead Pass and run due west from there to the Pacific Ocean. Construction started from both ends of the B.C. section in 1907, and the GTP founded its own cities at either end.

Near the railway's intended Pacific terminus there were two existing white settlements. One of them, Metlakatla, had lost most of its population to Alaska in 1887. The other, the small HBC centre first named Fort Simpson, then Port Simpson, was ignored by the railway, even though it had been chosen by Henry Cambie as the proposed terminus of the first transcontinental railway when he surveyed his line for the Canadian Pacific Railway from Yellowhead Pass in the 1870s. The GTP's choice was about twenty miles south of Port Simpson. Kaien Island was on an inside waterway well sheltered from the stormy western sea, but before anything could be done there, rock had to be blasted to fill the numerous muskeg swamps, a miserable task in a rain-filled climate. The GTP held a country-wide contest to choose a name for the new city at the railway's western terminus, and the winner (probably chosen to appease the disappointed fur traders), was the name of the fur company's first governor: Prince Rupert (see map "Rivers and a Railroad" in Chapter 1).[3]

At the eastern end of this huge railway project, the obvious site for a major centre was at the juncture of the two large rivers that dominate central British Columbia, the Fraser and the Nechako. The landowners in the two small settlements that were already there, Central and South Fort George, proposed a price holdup, so the railway set out its own township and called it Prince George. The often fog-filled basin where the rivers met was never a favourite spot for the Hudson's Bay men, who preferred the brighter shores of Stuart Lake, but the railway bowed to the inevitable.[4]

Premier Richard McBride immediately embraced this new development, as he had practised law in the coastal area of British Columbia, but he balked at the GTP's request for 6 million acres of provincial land as a resource to support the enterprise. He did agree to donate 10,000 acres of Kaien Island at a price of one dollar an acre. The government sold this land to an American railway contractor, who passed it on for what he paid for it to the GTP—and for services rendered, this contractor mysteriously and lavishly rewarded a Victoria lawyer and allegedly learned of other properties in the process. This strange procedure was never fully investigated. Robert Francis Green, McBride's minister responsible for railways, was forced to resign because he was part of that process. He was an excellent administrator, also in charge of public works. Both he and McBride were fully exonerated from any suspicion of benefiting personally. Green was eventually elected

South Fort George, seen here in 1914, was bypassed by the Grand Trunk Railroad when a new townsite to the north was surveyed by the Grand Trunk Pacific engineers.

In April 1914 Prince George held little but promise. By year end the size of its population was similar to that of South Fort George. The capital of the north would never look back.

At its peak in the 1880s Metlakatla was a thriving community dominated by William Duncan's "non-denominational Christian" church. Bitter infighting by church officials led to its demise, and a 1901 fire razed much of the community.

federally and in time became a senator, so he did not lose out. The only loser was the Department of Lands and Works, deprived of a good man at the helm by a railway before it was even built.[5]

From the start of inland exploration, the entrance to the Skeena Valley was from the ocean. As non-Native settlement spread slowly eastward, the white traveller transferred from coastal vessel to sternwheeler at Port Essington, a nice little town on the south side of the estuary, ten miles upstream from where the Skeena discharges into Chatham Sound.

The settlement owed its existence to Robert Cunningham, who founded it in 1870. He was a converted missionary and one of the first to leave William Duncan, the controversial and non-denominational Christian leader who had founded

Metlakatla. Cunningham left him in 1864, twenty-three years before Duncan fell out with the Anglican bishop and moved to Alaska with his flock. The churchman turned businessman worked for the Hudson's Bay Company for some years and then set up his own trading empire, starting with a store in Port Essington. This was just in the right spot to serve the sternwheelers that had followed the scent of gold and were moving miners and settlers inland to Hazelton. There the goldseekers set out to the Omineca goldfields, following the 40-mile-long trail to Babine Lake, with a 130-mile trip beyond that by Indian trails.[6]

Cunningham went into partnership with Thomas Hankin, a pioneer of the Hazelton area, and they opened a second trading post there. (The name Hazelton was rather late in coming; it was originally Skeena Forks.) A third enterprise of the venturesome pair was a contract with the provincial government to improve the trail from Hazelton to Babine Lake, a vital link for the pack trains and itinerant miners with whom they dealt.[7]

The groundbreaking theologian-cum-entrepreneur did not restrict his activities to trading posts and trail building; he went full tilt into water transportation, first with a steam tug operating from Metlakatla and Port Simpson to Port Essington, and then with two sternwheelers for service between Port Essington and Hazelton. One of these vessels was the highly regarded *Hazelton*.[8] Cunningham sent Captain J.H. Bonser to Victoria to design the boat and supervise its construction.[9]

The Skeena was the most difficult river in B.C. The weather problems of the Skeena Valley will be discussed at more length later, but in short: the river was subject to sudden heavy precipitation from the nearby Pacific, and therefore it rose and fell in level rapidly; its current was strong; and it was subject to continual winds. As will be recounted, wind gusts increased the danger of Kitselas Canyon, the Skeena's barrier to complacency for sternwheel skippers. The wind caused many of the accidents involving factors other than steam pressure, the most usual cause of disaster. The strong winds and fierce currents explain why more of its captains were the best.

The Skeena *went down to the lower Fraser River and was the last sternwheeler in service there. It died with its owner in 1925.*

The Danube, *shown here at Port Essington in about 1898, was owned by* *John Irving, who we will meet in Chapter 4.*

As in other parts of the province, the building of a railway first brought greatly increased business for the steamships, then none at all. One fine vessel, the *Skeena*, was built for the sole purpose of bringing beef to the railway crews; when that was over it was sent down to the Fraser River. Before the GTP shut down the river traffic, Cunningham's *Hazelton* was taken over by the Hudson's Bay Company, a latecomer, but rather a relentless one all the same.

The worst steamboat disaster on the Skeena occurred during this time in the Kitselas Canyon. It involved the HBC's *Mount Royal*, the *Hazelton*'s main competitor. Hit by a strong gust of wind in the canyon, the *Mount Royal* got crossways to the current, and six crewmen lost their lives when it capsized. Fortunately all the passengers were saved. The *Mount Royal* was replaced by the *Port Simpson*, a larger HBC vessel, which did most of its work below Kitselas Canyon, operating in conjunction with the *Hazelton*, which worked above it. (This was after the *Hazelton* was purchased by the HBC.)[10]

The Grand Trunk Pacific Railway left ample clearance for the largest sternwheelers, like the Omineca, *to pass under its bridge across the Skeena River at Skeena Crossing, but soon after this photo was taken in July 1912, the railway did away with the river traffic completely. This is the opposite approach but the same result as on the Fraser River upstream of Prince George, where the railway left no clearance for sternwheelers, whose owners desperately wished to continue service but could not pass under the bridges.*

The Grand Trunk Pacific Railway owners had a number of sternwheelers built, which they used in their own service and which they named with a total lack of imagination. Any grace departs when boats are called *Contractor*, *Operator*, and *Conveyor*. Only one was titled satisfactorily, the *Omineca*. After the railway was completed they all moved away or went to the scrapyard.

The last sternwheeler built for the Skeena was the fondly remembered *Inlander*, of so slight a draft that they used to say, "She could sail on anything a trifle moist." (The worst of these was the one that went, "A sternwheeler entered a stretch of low water and a passenger fell overboard and raised a cloud of dust."[11])The *Inlander* went into service in 1910, with Captain Bonser at the wheel (presumably after he had returned to the Skeena from the upper Fraser), and she served her local businessmen-owners very well indeed until 1912, when she was put to rest on the beach near Port Essington. By that year the

The Hazelton *lines her way past Ringbolt Island in Kitselas Canyon. Sternwheelers winched themselves through the canyon's turbulent waters using rings cemented into its walls. If you didn't want to brave the Skeena River by this means, your alternatives were a difficult canoe trip, with portages, a walk, or a sleigh ride on the ice in the winter until the Grand Trunk Pacific Railway was completed in 1911. It took another 33 years before there was a road.*

The Inlander *on the Skeena River at Kitselas Canyon. The pioneers were relieved as well as pleased to see the* Inlander *make it to Hazelton, as it always brought a supply of liquor.*

railway was in operation at its western end and was taking all the business, and once more the GTP put away the sternwheelers, leaving a district with no other means of transport than a railway and an inadequate road system.

In 1910, when things started moving not only on the railway but also around it, Port Essington was near to its fortieth birthday. It was a delightful little community with a fine townsite, an excellent harbour, and a backdrop of high mountains, usually snowclad, and it was close to the spectacular scenery of thirteen-mile-long Ecstall Inlet. The head of the inlet was the tidal access of the Ecstall River, which just a few miles upstream cascaded down Big Falls into the salt water. This was a hydro-electric resource made for the taking, but it did not realize its potential for another 30 years, by which time Port Essington's glitter was long gone. In spite of its advantages, the town was to suffer in the following years one of the most drawn-out departures ever listed in British Columbia's lengthy municipal death roll. Port Essington died because the railway was built on the other side of the Skeena's 2000-metre-wide estuary. The town lasted longer than the

This view of Port Essington shows its mountainous surroundings and fine harbour, c. 1908. Robert Cunningham (left) was the founder of Port Essington and a man not afraid to go from shopkeeping to water transportation and trail building, all part of his pioneer enterprise on the central coast of British Columbia. Below, his boat, Hazelton, *gets its teeth into the swift-flowing Skeena River.*

This picture was taken before the advent of the railway from Prince Rupert to Hazelton in 1911. It is unlikely that any kind of regular service was possible due to the unpredictability of the weather in the Skeena estuary. In the spring they would have to worry about ice above them (avalanches) and ice below them (thickness). The B.C. Provincial Police made the trip in the very worst of weather using dog teams.

paddlewheelers, but the end eventually came. The only monuments to Cunningham's lovely seaside base of operations after it disappeared completely in a forest fire in 1958 were the pylons crossing the Skeena to provide electricity to the city of Prince Rupert from generators powered by the Ecstall River.

Cunningham also set up a general store at Cedarvale, about 120 miles upstream from Port Essington and 60 miles downstream of Hazelton.[12] Cedarvale was the site of another Christian village, which was founded in 1888 and was originally named Minskinish. As its name indicates, Cedarvale lay among a handsome grove of cedars growing alongside the river. It occupied both banks of the river and was a good site for a ferry.

Minskinish was a settlement of the faith similar to Metlakatla. This latter was founded by William Duncan in 1862. Duncan had been sponsored in his Christian mission by the Royal Navy, which granted him passage and sustenance in a calculated move to pacify the coastal tribes by spreading the word of God. Duncan

Robert Tomlinson brought kindliness and dedication to his good work with the Native people at the Christian village he founded at Cedarvale in the Skeena Valley (originally called Minskinish). More tangible results came from the sawmill he built there. This is the Minskinish church in 1907.

was a stocky Yorkshireman, standing five feet four inches tall, with a black beard and a very independent nature. Before becoming a missionary he had been a leather salesman. He came out on the HMS *Satellite* in 1857[13] following the Haida's burning and plundering of the American schooner *Susan Sturges* at Masset in 1852.[14] After he moved his mission to Alaska in 1887, all help was withdrawn.

Minskinish was founded by missionary Robert Tomlinson after William Duncan left B.C. Tomlinson was not nearly as controversial a man of God as was his fellow churchman, though he was fully as enterprising and courageous and was a good friend to Duncan. He proved this in 1908 when he visited his colleague at New Metlakatla in Alaska, found him in need of assistance, and moved up there to help him. Tomlinson left his son in

Cedarvale, and Robert Junior continued a sawmilling operation, originally started in 1893, which for many years thereafter was the best in the area.[15]

Downstream from Cedarvale was the small village named Usk, about five miles upstream of Kitselas Canyon. This was where the *Mount Royal* capsized and sank in 1907.[16] For some reason the railway planners tried to make a population centre out of Usk, which acquired a hotel, a sawmill, and a general store, but they finally gave in to a more sensible development of the larger area around Terrace, another ten miles downstream. A ferry crossed the Skeena at Usk to connect with the road from Terrace. The railway ran on the right bank of the river, the road on the left.

Kitwanga, a large Native village, was upstream from Cedarvale, and a few miles farther along was Skeena Crossing, where the railway crossed to the left bank of the river ten miles downstream from Hazelton. It continued from there, passing south of Hazelton and proceeding east via the Bulkley Valley. The highway would later follow suit, also bypassing Hazelton.

The converging work crews came together on April 7, 1914, at Fraser Lake, where the last spike was driven, but the railway was already in trouble. Two years before, in April 1912, the GTP's first president, Charles Melville Hays, had gone down with the *Titanic*. Hays was returning from a money-raising trip to Europe, and his loss was a severe blow to an ill-conceived railway. Only two years after its triumphant opening, a declaration was made in the House of Commons that the Grand Trunk Pacific Railway was insolvent. Following an investigation by a royal commission, it became part of the publicly owned Canadian National Railway system in 1920. In 1933 it suffered the indignity of demotion from transcontinental to branch line. Ironically the City of Prince Rupert declared bankruptcy that same year.[17]

The GTP was a railway to nowhere in terms of the white settlers it reached; their numbers were tiny and they were spread very thinly along the edge of the rugged coastal wilderness. It is little wonder that it went bankrupt. It was a full quarter century

This view of the City of Prince Rupert, probably in the second or third decade of its life, shows its virtues and its vices. The fine harbour lies in the background, and in the foreground, spread out across the view, its least pleasant attribute, a muskeg swamp complete with stumps. Most houses were initially built on piles, as is the roadway on the far right.

With the GTP, as with the CPR, a forceful American was at the helm. Charles Melville Hays envisioned not only a railway, but also the city at its end, in this case Prince Rupert. After his great success with the Grand Trunk in the rest of Canada, where he turned deficit to profit, he was destined to leave the scene with the Titanic *before his B.C. project was half complete—and before it could be seen if he would have the same success with the Grand Trunk Pacific, a task of similar dimension to the ship in which he died.*

ahead of its time (almost exactly the same length of time it delayed the building of a continuous road connection from the mouth of the Skeena to the start of the inland plateau at Hazelton).

Construction cost overruns and mispractice probably also contributed to the bankruptcy. According to Russell R. Walker, who was manager of the North Coast Land Company in the Prince George area as well as the editor and publisher of the *Fort George Herald* newspaper, the Grand Trunk Railway in B.C. was originally estimated at $80 million but finally cost $120 million, due, he says, to a combination of poor estimating and to the "cost-plus" method of contracting. The main contract with Foley, Welch and Stewart across B.C. was a cost-plus one, and FW&S subcontracted widely. A cost-plus contract is one where the owner pays the contractor's actual costs and then an agreed percentage on top, the "plus." When the main contractor subcontracts, he usually keeps the plus for himself—if he does not also keep a part of the primary payment as well, as was often done.

Another source of problems with cost-plus contracting is that the more work the contractor does, the more profit he makes, so without close control, more work than is really necessary often takes place. This sometimes includes totally ineffective operations. Walker writes that he observed work crews building a tunnel at Hansard, near Upper Fraser, in soft material that could not be stabilized. This operation was obviously futile. He commented that this happened because "cost-plus contracts were so nice to come home to," and that the profits taken by FW&S were "fabulous." The company also profited greatly by overcharging its employees for outfitting, room, and board, and the men said that FW&S stood for "Frig'em, Work'em, and Starve'em."[18]

The final cost quoted by Walker compares well with a more official one of $140 million for the Prince Rupert to Edmonton section of the GTP. The amount of the overrun was also believable because the eastern section of the railway, that within the rest of Canada, was estimated originally at $60 million and came out at $160 million.[19] (It is conceivable that the dominion government

CHAIRS IN THE BEER PARLOUR AND
HYMNBOOKS IN THE PEWS

In 1957 the author visited the Skeena West highways district. District superintendent Carl Shaw suggested a trip by small boat to Port Essington, where the district still had some road and sidewalk maintenance responsibilities. It was a beautiful summer afternoon, and the Skeena estuary was in one of its infrequent benign moods. After parking by the roadside at Tyee—ensuring that there was sufficient clearance for a train to pass—we scrambled down the rock fill to the river's edge.

Soon the small motor launch that we had rented approached with its operator, and we set off across that always impressive river. En route we gazed at the rather weird sight of a tall high-tension power line pylon that seemed to ride on the water but was actually supported on piles. The crossing was three kilometres and took about half an hour. We steered straight out, directly across the current, and the river carried us downstream just enough to make a landing at Port Essington dock in good time.

The dock was typical of hundreds on the coast, and behind it was a building that was also unremarkable, two storeys faced with grey cedar planking and evidently a hotel, but one no longer in use. The small collection of buildings was absolutely deserted. In the sunshine with the blue sky behind there was only the hum of bees. As we crossed we had come by the opening of Ecstall Inlet, about 800 metres wide, and the view, with steep mountain slopes on either side of the azure water, was breathtakingly beautiful. It was almost an exact reproduction of the glimpse you catch looking up Jervis Inlet toward Prince of Wales Reach from the ferry between Earl's Cove and Saltery Bay on the lower coast. Both inlets are similar in width.

We walked over to the hotel. The front windows were unboarded and we looked into the beer parlour, where we saw that the chairs were still in place. It was as if someone had simply walked out and locked the door. There was a board sidewalk alongside the road surface. Shaw said the road had also been planked until it became unsafe. The sidewalk was full of dry rot.

Through the trees we spotted a small wooden church, which we decided to visit. The wooden walkway to it was even more rotted and overgrown, and walking was hazardous. The door of the church was open, the organ stood in the corner, the pews remained in fine shape, and the hymnbooks were still in place. We touched nothing and took nothing. We were very thoughtful as we walked back to the boat.

The next summer, in a prolonged dry spell, a forest fire bore down on Port Essington. The bone-dry wooden sidewalks carried the flames throughout the town, which was completely incinerated, including the hotel and the church.

Construction crew using a track-layer on the GTP Railway near Kitselas, about 1910. As the CPR's Andrew Onderdonk did in the Fraser Canyon, Charles Hays built his own dynamite factory to meet the GTP's blasting needs. His factory was on Wolf Island in Prince Rupert Harbour and it produced ten million pounds of explosives. Unlike Onderdonk, Hays did not blow his up.

condoned blocking navigation on the Fraser, as described in the previous chapter, to avoid adding to the overruns and delays with redesigned and much more expensive bridging.)

Foley, Welch and Stewart tried its hand at an initial contract for the PGE Railway south from Prince George. The largesse of the dominion government was not available for this, however, and the contract was eventually dropped by mutual agreement with the provincial government due to the dearth of funding during the wartime recession. That area had to wait another 35 years for rails (see Chapter 3).

In course of time the GTP turned out to be a wonderful thing for central and northern British Columbia west of Prince George. For one thing, it consolidated the white population's grip on the coast. For another, it completely changed the transportation pattern across the interior plateau from Hazelton east to Prince George. Instead of following lake and river, the railway followed the route of the Collins Overland Telegraph line straight across the Nechako Plateau in favourable terrain westwards, through the lake country around Burns Lake, and then by the Bulkley River valley to Hazelton until it met the mountains. The settlement it encouraged was much easier to serve by road than anything that would have come from the fur traders' way of travel by water. The railway planners were wise to follow the Nechako Valley. Although none of these lands ever achieved the agricultural potential forecast, there was good farming country as far as Smithers; a huge timber resource all the way through; a rather late-arriving mineral wealth; and an abundance of hydro-electric potential.

On the other hand, the construction of the railroad was a fatal blow to any hopes the residents of the area may have had for a road beside the lower Skeena. No one could envisage a roadway sharing the steep rock bluffs, which stretched for 60 miles alongside the river between Kaien Island and Terrace, with the track. For the first several decades after the railway appeared, all the small settlements that came with it were accessed by it; roads to them were of minimum quality and for local access only.

And the train was not always a reliable method of access. Alex Lord, the pioneer B.C. school inspector, describes a trip he started out on from Prince Rupert to Prince George on the GTP in May 1916. After a delay of two days at Kitwanga due to trouble on the line, they reached Hazelton where the conductor informed them, "There are forty slides in forty miles ahead." Five days later the GTP brought in another train and offered free transportation back to Prince Rupert and by boat down to Vancouver, which Lord accepted. He later heard that the passengers who stayed on did not reach Edmonton until 30 days after they left Prince Rupert—

These passengers are enjoying the scenery from the viewing platform at the back of a Grand Trunk Pacific train, one of the first to run between Prince Rupert and Hazelton in 1911, three years before the line was complete across B.C. to Yellowhead Pass. This run was enough to put the sternwheelers out of business completely on that section. The photograph was taken at Mile 45, about midway between Prince Rupert and Terrace. It demonstrates what the line had to fear from mountain runoff.

The trip made by B.C.'s school inspector/author Alex Lord in May 1917 would have given passengers lots of time to admire the mountains.

The lower photo shows the first transcontinental passenger train arriving in Prince Rupert in April 1914.

something of a record! Delays of several days on the trip, which was supposedly biweekly, were regular from then on.[20]

Some time later in its life, road was built alongside this railway through the lower Skeena Valley, one of the most difficult areas for roadbuilding in British Columbia. It was constructed in great urgency during World War II, and that road would not have been built had the railway not been there first. Conversely, the building of the road would have been much easier had the railway *not* been there. Added to nature's intransigence was that of the railwaymen, who most definitely did not want a road.

When the Japanese attacked Pearl Harbour in December 1941, there was no continuous roadway from Prince Rupert to Terrace, nor from Terrace to Hazelton. The Japanese attack, and the subsequent declaration of war on that country by the United States and Canada, gave every outlet to the Pacific Ocean an importance it had never previously held: that of continental defence.

It was the least admirable quality of the climate around the Skeena River—"the river of clouds" as the Native people called it—which led to its first recognition as a potential wartime transportation artery. When an American troop transport en route from Seattle to Alaska ran aground in a period of zero visibility in 1942, it was refloated and towed into Prince Rupert for repairs. The military officer in charge was greatly impressed when he realized how much the ocean voyage would be reduced if they were to move troops and supplies by train to Prince Rupert from American centres. The Canadian and American governments agreed, and a large American army transit camp was set up on the east shore of Kaien Island where the village of Port Edward lies today. Troop trains rumbled along the Skeena Valley. All that was needed as a backup to the railway was a road, and action was taken at once to solve that problem.[21]

In early March 1942 seven twelve-man survey parties set out along the Skeena River under the direction of Canada's Department of Mines and Resources, financed by the Canadian and American governments. Two stretches of very difficult terrain awaited them

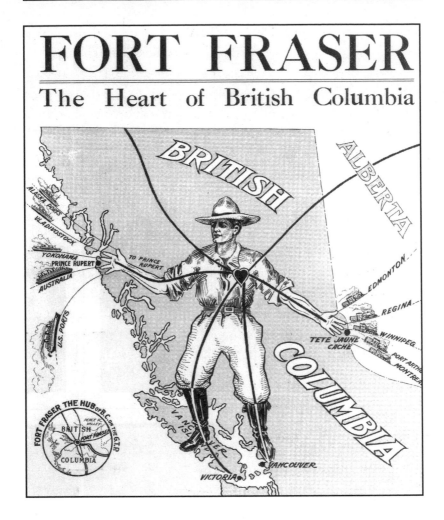

With the building of the Grand Trunk Pacific, even abandoned Hudson's Bay Company forts became land promotions for developers. This heart of B.C. is today a dot on the map 150 kilometres west of Prince George.

in the areas where they sought to build a road—the 70 miles from Tyee to Terrace, and 20 miles between Usk and Kitwanga.

That the provincial Department of Public Works could find neither men nor money to undertake this survey shows how low the B.C. provincial economy was due to wartime conditions. The DPW only provided the party chiefs; the dominion government supplied the rest—the staff to supervise construction, as well as the crews and resources to undertake the construction. In the section between Tyee and Terrace, the Canadian National Railway was right alongside the route proposed for the road, and it became heavily involved in the actual road construction. For once in its existence it might have shown a profit. The construction method used was to quarry rock and dump it on the outer side of the railway grade to form a road grade, in many cases using rail cars to move it. The railway co-operated. There was a war on.

By 1944 the link was complete through both parts. By modern standards it was not much of a road, simply a widening of the rail grade, about twenty feet wide at most, running very close to the railway and the steep rock bluffs, and usually with the wide, deep river on the other side. Unwary drivers who strayed from the road surface, exhausted by the long miles, went into the river. But there was a road, and the army convoys could get through.[22]

One reason for the road's bad reputation initially was the railway's refusal to permit the road authority to build in proper superelevation, or banking, on those curves where the road surface would slope towards the track. At these places the road had no banking at all, which is not a safe driving condition. "Superelevation" or "banking" are road engineering terms that refer to the practice of inclining the surface of the road laterally around a curve, inner side downwards, to make it easier to drive at speed. It often turned out that those curves without superelevation were the most dangerous anyway, surrounded by the steepest cliffs. To meet a thundering train suddenly on one of these sections was an experience that was not easily forgotten. The ban on trackward-sloping superelevation was dropped in 1955.

The tunnel at Kwinitsa Bluff. In 1956 the Canadian National Railway, the inheritor of the Grand Trunk Pacific Railway, decided to move its rail line outside the tunnel along the bank of the river. The provincial Department of Public Works immediately had to rebuild the road out into the river. Note how close the rail grade is to the highway pavement.

Driving the road was always an interesting exercise, especially on a dry summer day when washboard and dust made conditions even more miserable. Roadside stops could also be exciting due to the narrowness of the road and the close proximity of the track. Everyone wanted to park on the side of the road away from the river. It was easy to underestimate clearances from the nearby track, and no train was about to stop if there was not enough room for it to go by. In the 1950s, trainloads of logs kept the railway going. These were hauled on flatcars. The logs were unchained and rather haphazardly piled between infrequent uprights. As the logs were long and not at all straight, it was not uncommon for a butt-end to protrude for a foot or two more than normal. It was also not unknown for one or more of these logs to fall off. On one occasion the author was parked beside the track to examine roadside

This scene of the GTP track by the Skeena River in its lower reaches shows one of the few places where the road is on the other side of the track from the river. It also shows that the terrain on the far side of the Skeena was no less difficult for building than that on the railway side. An even worse detriment was its northern exposure.

erosion when he suddenly became aware of such an overwidth train approaching. A Department of Highways record for the 100-yard dash was established.

Despite all of this, the roadbuilding was a remarkable achievement, one that was not made known to the people of the province at the time due to wartime security. It was built in terrain as difficult as any found in British Columbia, not only along the widened river in its estuary, but up the narrow and difficult valley to Hazelton.

A glance at the map shows numerous large streams flowing into the Skeena, and their names ring nicely to the ear—Khyex, Exchamsiks, Exstew, Zimacord, Kitsumkalum, Zymoetz, Kleanza, and Chimdemash. All of these required very substantial bridges with main spans of 200 feet or more. A short note in Bridge Engineer G.M. Duncan's annual report for fiscal year 1942-43 states:

The staff was engaged in preparing plans for the bridges on the Prince Rupert-Terrace-Cedarvale Highway for the Dominion Government. Plans for eleven bridges had to be made, including those for a 225-foot span timber Howe truss, which is the longest yet designed in the office.

This modest statement covers the designing of some of the finest timber road bridges ever built, wooden structures using the superior strength of Douglas fir. These bridges lasted well into the 1970s. The Terrace area receives heavy annual snowfalls—it is not unusual for up to 40 inches to fall in 24 hours, immediately followed by heavy rain—and the bridges had to be designed to carry a very heavy snow loading. This deadload capacity made them capable of carrying the heaviest of logging trucks when clear of snow, which turned out to be a great benefit to the area's major industry. All in all, 39 bridges were added to the bridge register between Prince Rupert and Cedarvale.

Considering the difficulty of this construction and the absolute necessity of the railway's complete co-operation, it is doubtful that there would have been a road there as early as 1944 had the government and the national emergency not intervened. That they did not have a road before this was not from want of trying, and one notable roadbuilder had done his best sixteen years earlier.

In 1928 W.G. Gwyer, a civil engineer of the B.C. Department of Public Works, was moved to Prince Rupert as district engineer. He was a man not lacking in imagination, and in an innovative attempt to find an alternate route for a road from Prince Rupert to Terrace, he advertised across Canada for an aviator capable of flying over the Coast Mountains to make an aerial survey. This proposal was much ahead of its time. The replies filed in Victoria make interesting reading. In the DPW Annual Report for the fiscal year 1929-30, Gwyer writes:

> What I consider one of the most important projects undertaken during the season was the aerial survey to determine the feasibility of a route from Prince Rupert

Terrace may not have the worst weather in British Columbia (and that is debatable), but its claim to the most varied is well founded. Two wide openings through the mountains from the Pacific—the lower Skeena Valley and the Douglas Channel—converge above the town. This geographical feature affects the weather, producing systems that can sometimes bring as much as 40 inches of snow in 24 hours. The snow can change instantaneously to heavy rain that can go on indefinitely. Some makes of prefabricated buildings are built to snow-loading standards that cannot accept the challenge of Terrace weather, and occasionally they demonstrate this flaw by collapsing. The snowfall on the Khyex Bridge, shown above, is true to form. The bridge can withstand the weight, but the snow must be removed as soon as possible, and this must not be done with heavy equipment. Human power is best.

East of Terrace through to the summit of the first interior range near Cedarvale, rain can be accompanied by freezing temperatures. In such circumstances, a motorist driving at speed may encounter rain water that has turned to ice on top of a packed snow surface. This ice will spin a car and often flip it on its roof. Motorists in the early days, before the advent of such things as radios, improved highways, and radio-operated digital signs, took a chance—it was the spin of the wheel!

east, other than following the Skeena River. A series of
photographs taken conclusively proved that the reports
of a hidden pass were a fallacy. The next step in this
direction was to make a reconnaissance survey to find out
the best possible route to a point on the Skeena River as
far as it was possible to go east without interference with
the railway, the object being to find a ferry crossing. This
project is still under investigation.

The record shows that Gwyer paid the dauntless aviator
$2227.37 for his work. In that rain-drenched wilderness there are
many peaks and ridges over 2000 metres in height. The mountains
north of the Skeena are an unbroken barrier for 50 miles to the
Nass. The Skeena Valley is the only slot through them.[23]

It does not take very much reading between the lines, either
in the Department of Public Works annual reports of that time or
in the correspondence files, to come to the conclusion that the
CNR right-of-way was out-of-bounds to the highway authority
before the last war. The words "without interference to the railway"
in the above quote certainly indicate that. No thought was given
to building around the west coast of Kaien Island alongside the
railway to Zenardi Rapids, despite that being an area containing
numerous large fish-canning operations that eventually would
need road access. The roadbuilders in the 1920s ran into serious
difficulties on the route they were forced to take on the eastern
side of the island to a crossing at Galloway Rapids. (Galloway and
Zenardi rapids are the two narrowest channels separating Kaien
Island from the mainland; both are subject to strong tidal currents.)
In the annual reports of 1926 and 1927 the following comments
appear:

> Most of the subgrade of this road is muskeg, the surface
> being carried on rafts of various designs to suit conditions...
>   Approximately five miles of this road had to be carried
> on cedar planking close-laid on muskeg.

The centre of Kaien Island was obviously not an easy place in which to build a road, but the southern narrows and the coastal route to it were pre-empted by the railway.

During the wonderfully active years of early roadbuilding in British Columbia from 1922 to 1929, the Department of Public Works did its best to extend the road along the Skeena River valley east of Terrace. Here the railway had the preferred side of the valley, that with a southern exposure. The road was built on the other side from the railway, despite the settlement and industry springing up beside the tracks. The roadbuilders had great difficulty

Road of close-laid logs at Prince Rupert. When the authorities undertook the construction of roads and streets on Kaien Island, the site the railway planners chose for their terminal city on the West Coast, they found that they had to take special measures to deal with the deep muskeg (a Cree word meaning bog or swamp). There were really only two alternatives: either excavate and haul away the soft material and substitute shot rock of sufficient depth that it would lock together to form a base (a very expensive solution but nevertheless the one finally used); or float the roadway across. The cheapest way to do this was to use small logs tied together as shown above.

with soil and snow conditions due to the lack of sunlight in that narrow valley, and they failed to complete a lasting and reliable road for many years. They also, in order to gain contact with the various settlements on the right bank of the river, had to put in numerous reaction ferries to serve both sides of the valley.

At one time there were a total of nine ferries crossing the Skeena in the 120-mile stretch between Tyee and Kitwanga. These were reduced to five by the 1920s and to two by the 1970s. For a few years there was a ferry at Copper City, which is at the confluence of the Skeena with the Zymoetz River (also known as the Copper River, this is the first stream upriver from Terrace, flowing in from the east), but that soon went out of service.

A bridge at river level soon replaced the ferry at Hazelton. This was joined by the handsome high-level Hagwilget Suspension Bridge across the Bulkley River in 1930, a favourite of photographers ever since (Hagwilget Canyon is immediately upstream of Hazelton). That same year a 200-foot-span timber Howe truss bridge was built at Galloway Rapids to connect Kaien Island by road to the mainland.

In 1925 an elegant, multiple-span steel bridge was built at Terrace across the Skeena River—its deck was made of timber, which had to be replaced constantly. It made two ferries unnecessary, the ones at Remo and Terrace. In the 1950s the Highways department was forced to accept a railway bridge at the same site and in very close proximity to its bridge when a spur line went in to Kitimat. This resulted in a very unsafe same-level crossing.

The ferries at Kitselas, Pacific (a railway point midway between Usk and Cedarvale), and from Tyee to Port Essington were gone by the 1940s. The remaining ferries at Usk and Cedarvale saw service for many years, but today the ferry at Usk alone survives.

The Kitselas Canyon was only a short distance downstream of the Cedarvale ferry, so one of the responsibilities of the ferry operator was to look out for small boats or others in distress or in danger of drifting downstream and to rescue them. One year during the spring flood the operator saw what he thought was a

The ferry at Cedarvale, shown here, was immediately upstream of Kitselas Canyon. The ferry operator ran a rescue service for craft or people caught in the current.

pile of logs approaching with a man on top of them. It was in fact a load of logs with the logging truck still attached to it by its load chains, the whole rig drifting down towards the canyon with the vehicle under water. The truck had gone off the road a few miles upstream, and the truckdriver quickly abandoned his cab and climbed on top of his load. The driver jumped when he passed the ferry, and the captain rescued him. The logs came loose in the canyon and they made it through, but the truck went to the bottom and joined the *Mount Royal*, which had been waiting there for company for over 50 years.

Despite the work put in to make it usable all year round, in 1956 the road between Hazelton and Terrace was closed for over three weeks to all traffic due to almost bottomless mud from a very bad spring breakup. Many stalled motorists had to put up at

A LIGHT BY THE DOOR AT CEDARVALE

It was a road nobody loved during the 1950s and most of the 1960s—a twisting, winding snake through a narrow, steep-sided mountain valley, 45 miles of dust in summer and shadowed ice and snow in winter—the Terrace to Cedarvale stretch. The only logic to its alignment when it opened in 1944 was that it took the easiest path, and that was not the straightest. Lack of clearing, the narrow width of roadway, and its poor alignment, combined with its climate, made it a wonderful snow-trap for the unwary motorist. As the Northern Trans-Provincial Highway was progressively improved from Prince George westwards after the last war, pavement slowly crept towards tidewater, but the Terrace to Cedarvale stretch saw neither hide nor hair of a paving machine for over twenty years.

The narrow slash through the dense forest carried the only road from Terrace and Prince Rupert to the rest of British Columbia. As the area awakened in the last years of the 1950s with the advent of Kitimat, inter-regional road traffic was encouraged by the improvements and paving of the route from Smithers eastward. Prior to that all traffic was by ship, air, or (of course) rail. Travelling salesmen and the odd visiting civil servant now tried driving through in winter. If they left Prince Rupert in the morning and made calls in Terrace after lunch, it was already darkening when they drove east over the Terrace to Cedarvale stretch.

Smithers was the goal for overnight, and there was absolutely no settlement at roadside from Terrace to Cedarvale. The Grand Trunk Pacific railway planners had decreed this when they built their track on the other side of the Skeena River in 1911. What the weary eastbound driver craved to see, as the long miles dragged by and the roadside snowbanks crowded in, was the lights of Cedarvale, the first human habitation by the road in 45 miles. The lights of the Cedarvale cafe and gas station were always on. When he saw them, the tired motorist could only murmur quietly, "Thank God."

The coffee was always hot and the news of road conditions and weather was always true. Even at four in the morning the motorist in need of aid found a light on by the front door, and a knock on the door always brought someone. Robert Tomlinson the missionary, secure in paradise, was surely warmed by the benevolence that continued in this corner of Canada's northwest where in 1887 he brought to life the small Christian village of Minskinish and nurtured it so carefully.

A glance at a relief map of the Prince Rupert area shows a huge Y on its side with its arms pointing toward the sea. The right arm of the Y is the wide lower Skeena Valley; the left arm is the equally wide opening of Douglas Channel leading to the Kitimat Valley and over Lakelse Lake. The two arms meet at Terrace, where the upper Skeena Valley running inland to Hazelton forms the bottom leg of the Y, and there lies the Terrace to Cedarvale stretch.

In 1966 the Department of Highways reported, "The Northern Trans-Provincial Highway west of Prince George is now bituminous surfaced, with the exception of thirty miles in the Pacific/Kitwanga area east of Terrace." (Pacific was the name of a CNR division point, a dot on the map ten miles upstream of Usk.) The last section of the inter-regional highway system in B.C. to be rebuilt was the one with the worst weather regime in the province.

But progress was on the way, and as the 1960s ended the trees were cut back and the forest no longer crowded in. The road grade was widened and lifted, and snowbanks never formed thereafter—the high-speed plough trucks rolled quickly on the smooth blacktop and blasted the snow well back on the wide right-of-way. Cars sped by rapidly, even in the worst of winter weather, and certainly in darkness. Most of them probably never even noticed the cafe and gas station by the grove of cedars.

An era had come to an end, and there was no more need for the light by the door at Cedarvale.

However, the Department of Highways could not change the weather. On the last day of November 1978, the storms flowing in from the Pacific along the arms of the Y brought rain that did not fall in drops. It came down from the sky in waves of water. That night every drainage channel in the area of the Y turned into a chocolate-brown torrent, and with the roar of boulders in the flow you could not hear yourself talk within a hundred feet of a creek. By far the worst area was the bottom leg of the Y where all this came to rest. Every drainage structure and bridge on the highway from Terrace to Cedarvale suffered damage that night, some worse than others and many disappeared completely.

the one and only motel in the Terrace area at that time, appropriately named The Motel, and their description of the road was unprintable. This road had to wait until the 1970s before it was brought up to full standard and paved.

For a few years after it was built, the Prince Rupert to Terrace highway was not opened to traffic in winter. This situation was due mostly to the snowploughing methods of the railway. The railroaders saw no reason why they should not plough snow at will from their track over onto the roadway. Large snowslides or avalanches are quite frequent in this area in some winters, and the most predictable of these was at Kwinitsa Bluff. Every spring the district engineer would wait until the Kwinitsa slide came down before he opened the road. The road was first opened in winter in 1948 and it has been open every winter since then.

For twenty years after the war the highway along the lower Skeena cliffs remained relatively unchanged, except for a gradually increasing mileage of paved surface. It was rare that a traveller on the road did not meet trucks dumping shot rock over the road edge as ballast to offset the river's constant erosion. In the late 1960s and early 1970s the replacement of the fine old bridges commenced, starting with Galloway Rapids. This required extensive road relocations, and these were built to modern standards and linked together. By the late 1980s there was a new highway, twice the width of the original and most of it well clear of the railway, with guard rails between them.

Since January 1974, when a roadside cafe and gas station near Shames was wiped out and seven people lost their lives, the Department of Highways has monitored avalanches in the area. The vicious winter weather sweeping in from the Pacific Ocean can bring whiteouts and blizzards along with avalanches. The stalwart men maintaining road and rail in this part of the province regard these onslaughts of nature quite simply as added problems.

The Galloway Rapids Bridge joined Kaien Island to the mainland as part of the Yellowhead Highway. It was built in 1930, and the structure shown was replaced by a steel and concrete span in 1975. It was a model for most of the eleven wooden bridges designed by the Department of Public Works in 1942 for the many river crossings on the road from Prince Rupert through to Terrace, these being built during World War II and paid for in the emergency by the governments of Canada and the United States. The major difference from the model in those built later was the use of creosote to treat the timbers for longevity. Classic Douglas fir structures, these Howe truss bridges gave stalwart service. As well as that shown, bridges crossed the Skeena at various large tributary streams including Zimacord (225-foot span, a record in B.C. for a timber span), Exchamsiks, Exstew, Khyex, and Kitsumkalum Rivers. These bridges were originally intended as two lane, but later in their long lives were restricted to single lane for loaded trucks when truckloads became heavier. Their built-in strength to resist the extremely heavy snow loading of the area paid off because they could accommodate modern logging trucks. All of these wartime bridges were replaced by steel and concrete structures in the mid-1970s.

Section Two

Northern British Columbia from the Nass River and the Peace River to the Yukon and the Northwest Territory

Chapter 3

British Columbia East of the Rockies

*Peculiar people promote the Peace—
and the road that finally arrives in wartime
goes north rather than west or south*

When the powers that be drew out the new Canadian province of British Columbia on the map in 1871, they marked out the eastern boundary by coming up the continental divide from the 49th parallel to its intersection with the 120-degree west meridian. Then they followed that line on the map from there on to the 60th parallel, which was the northern limit. Whether these were the same dimensions as for the colony prior to confederation is debatable. Some say that when the boundaries of the British Empire's second colony on the west coast of North America were set in 1858, the watershed of the Finlay River marked the northeast corner.

When Surveyor-General Joseph Trutch drew a map of the colony in 1871, he showed the 120-degree meridian as the continuation of the eastern border from the continental divide, with a note on the meridian line "Boundary of British Columbia 1866," that being the year when the colony was greatly enlarged by the addition of Vancouver Island. It is possible that an adjustment was made then. On the other hand, the surveyor-general's wonderful effort at charting the colony is quite noticeably inaccurate in places. It only goes as far north as the 56th parallel for one thing, and it shows Fort St. John as being east of the 120-degree meridian, which would put it in Alberta—though many in that city have wished that it were east of that meridian rather than west of it![1]

Whatever the boundaries of the colony were, the new province gained about 70,000 square miles in the area acquired east of the Rockies that reached far into the almost totally desolate north and east and was about as distant as possible from the provincial capital. This area beyond the Rocky Mountains was promptly forgotten in Victoria and remained that way for about the first 80 years of the life of Canada's westernmost province.

The shape of this addition of land resembled an ear, and that might be a suitable metaphor for it. It could be called a third ear, and like such an unnecessary addition it had a good use within itself, but it was so difficult to comfortably attach it to the whole that it might have been better to have passed it by in the first place. The Peace River area, and the area north of it, had no overland connection at all to the rest of B.C. for that period of 80 years. It was not until 1952, when the Hart Highway was opened between Prince George and Dawson Creek, that British Columbians could drive to it within their own province, and it was another six years before they could ride there in a train within B.C.

The only easy route into the area from B.C. was via the Peace River, and that was full of rapids and only navigable by canoes, which could be portaged, until it reached Hudson Hope. The result was that until 1952, the lifeline to the southern part of the area was within Alberta (originally part of the Northwest Territory). To complicate things even further for the Ear, early in its life Ottawa arranged to take over administration and settlement of the land in the Peace River Block as payment for its investment in the Canadian Pacific Railway. The Peace River Block contained much of the best land suitable for agriculture in the area, and this was now estranged from the B.C. government, which promptly turned its back on the entire area.[2]

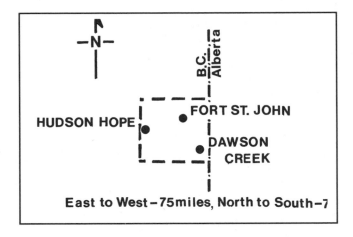

The Peace River Block

The Peace River Block, as defined in March 1912, was a rectangle, 5250 square miles or 3.36 million acres in area (although I have seen it referred to as 3.5 million acres). The Peace River, flowing from west to east, more or less bisected the western and eastern boundaries. In an eighteen-month period in 1928-29 the block doubled its population, from 3000 to 6000, and it continued to grow steadily until the Great Depression settled in, at which time 85 percent of the farmers went on relief. The Block was returned to British Columbia for settlement in 1930. Prior to that the land had been taken by the national government in restitution for lands it had given up to the Canadian Pacific Railway.

The centre named Dawson Creek was born when the Northern Alberta Railway decided to terminate its track there. The first train rolled into Dawson Creek in January 1931.

The history of the Ear reflects this attitude of abandonment, especially in respect to transportation. Its history became a story of visitations rather than of continuing developments. The first visitation was of course that of Alexander Mackenzie, accompanied by Alexander Mackay, six picked voyageurs, and a specially built 25-foot birchbark canoe. They passed through in 1793 on their way to the Pacific coast, but Mackenzie did not linger either on the way in or on the way back. His trip started and ended in Fort Chipewyan on Lake Athabasca, taking a total time of three and a half months.

He was followed by his fellow North Wester Simon Fraser in 1805. Fraser used the Peace River as his way through the mountains (a route eventually called the Peace River Gap), but very soon

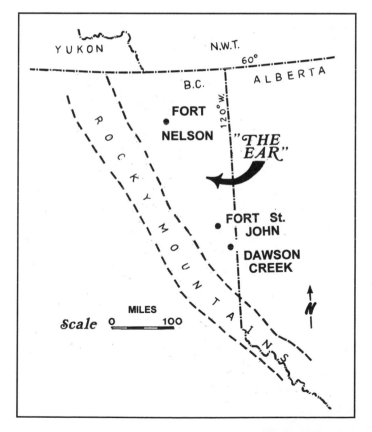

Northeast British Columbia—the "Ear"

after that he switched to Leather Pass (later called Yellowhead Pass). This led him from Jasper's House to McLeod's Lake near the headwaters of the Parsnip River, and later to Fort St. James and the rest of New Caledonia (see the map "Rivers of Northeast British Columbia"). After it purchased the North West Company, the Hudson's Bay Company was also busy in the area, with outposts at Hudson Hope, Fort St. John, Fort Nelson, and a remote one at Dease Lake, as well as others even more remote. The one thing that these outposts had in common was that they were all peripheral to the four western fur districts, or departments, of the Hudson's Bay Company, which were New Caledonia, the Columbia, Athabasca, and the Mackenzie Basin.

Aside from the comings and goings of the fur traders, nothing much happened until excitement arose about the transcontinental railway route in the early 1870s. A former Hudson's Bay Company man named Charles Horetzky was in charge of the most northern survey for Sanford Fleming, seeking the longed-for railway route. He confirmed the existence of Pine Pass, previously only known to the Natives, although Mackenzie was told of it. Lying between the headwaters of Misinchinka Creek, a tributary of the Parsnip River, and the Pine River, a larger stream flowing eastwards and more directly into the Peace, the pass is located about fifty miles south of the Gap.[3]

Lowly Misinchinka Creek gave its name to the Misinchinka Range of the Rocky Mountains, and Pine Pass is a way through that range at 2992 feet above sea level, which is the lowest crossing of the Rockies in Canada. Horetzky extended his line westwards to Takla Lake and by the upper Skeena valley to the Nass and the Pacific coast by that opening. It was a very good route, but one that was unacceptable because it was too far north. Horetzky's route through Pine Pass was followed by the Hart Highway in the 1950s and by the British Columbia Railway a few years after that.

A pronounced lack of the resources necessary to support life was one reason the area remained unsettled for so long. It was a country that would kill people, either by the distances combined

The Peace River Canyon is the impassable barrier to any continuous use of the Peace River as a waterway through the Rocky Mountains, although it is east of them by a few miles. In the early 1930s a group of river boatmen from the Finlay River conducted an experiment by strongly bracing a 25-foot wooden river boat and setting it off, with no crew, from their river down the Peace. All that they recovered at the mouth of the canyon were rather small pieces, one with the name of the boat on it. Within the Rockies lie the Finlay rapids and the Ne Parle Pas rapids, the latter so named, as Warburton Pike said, "from the absence of the roar of water which usually gives warning." They are navigable by skilled boatmen with care. The canyon requires a twelve-mile portage.

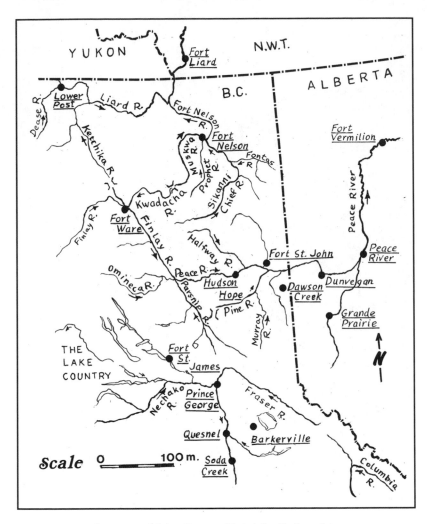

Rivers of Northeast British Columbia

The Vermilion Chutes are off the map, about 50 miles downstream of Fort Vermilion.

   The elevation of Sifton Pass at the head of the Ketchika and Fox rivers is 3274 feet (998 metres). Pine Pass, at the head of the Pine River, is 2992 feet (912 metres). The Bedaux Pass is at the head of the Muskwa and Kwadacha rivers, beside Fern Lake (named for Mrs. Bedaux), and is 4500 feet (1372 metres) in elevation.

with bitter cold and constant winds, or by the dearth of sustenance, or both. It lacked the salmon resource of the lands across the mountains, and the northern buffalo and other game were often not there when they were most needed as a source of food. That redoubtable English big-game hunter, Warburton Pike, who is more fully discussed in Chapter 4, came close to the ultimate decision during the winter of 1890-91, when his party ran out of supplies and could find nothing to shoot. (The ultimate decision is whether to face a painful death by starvation or to stave it off by consuming your companions once they become deceased.) Pike and his party finally staggered into Hudson Hope more dead than alive, and they were lucky the Hudson's Bay Company was there.[4]

After that, very little happened, although during the Klondike incursion, circa 1898, some hardy souls tried to reach the gold fields by way of the Peace River Gap, up the Rocky Mountain Trench via the Finlay valley, and over what became known as Sifton Pass into the Liard watershed. They then crossed over another divide to Teslin Lake and the Teslin River. After that it was more or less clear sailing, or drifting, to Dawson City. It was not a bad route, better than many.

Then in 1913, 1934, and 1942, three quite remarkable visitations occurred.

Very likely the first owed its genesis to Warburton Pike, one more example of big-game hunters in British Columbia at the end of the century passing on word to their homeland of the wonders of the Canadian west. On his visit, Pike must have noticed the existence of coal in that area, as he was a man aware of the value of minerals. One person who heard the word and came out to see for himself was a man named D.A. Thomas, a wealthy coal tycoon from Wales, who eventually was titled Lord Rhonnda. His visit occurred in 1913. (His peerage came later, the result of his work as controller of Britain's national food supplies during World War I.)

Thomas not only conceived a major coal-producing area for the upper Peace at Hudson Hope, he also noted indications of oil and gas near Fort Vermilion, a few hundred miles downstream on

BEAR WITH IT

The historical lack of big game in the Peace and Pine river valleys was not always the case. One morning in the early 1960s a rancher, whose place was located near the East Pine Ferry close to the town of Chetwynd, was awakened by suspicious noises from his cattle. He was a single man, living alone. Picking up his rifle, which as usual was fully loaded, he rounded the side of his cabin and came upon a very large grizzly bear crouched over a steer, which it had just killed. On his approach the animal reared up, standing on its hind legs with its front paws extended above its head, the claws on them fully visible. It towered above him.

The man's reaction was immediate: he raised his rifle and fired repeatedly, aiming for the upper chest and neck of the huge animal, levering shell after shell into the chamber. Fortunately one of these shells hit a vital spot and the bear died as it dropped toward him, and as he jumped to the side.

The rancher, fearing the presence of other bears, did not stay around. He drove to Chetwynd for coffee and breakfast at the hotel to sustain himself. There he met a road survey crew, who were also breakfasting, and the author, who was visiting them. The breathless bear-killer regaled them with a dramatic story of his encounter. Their curiosity fully aroused, the whole road crew set off down the side road to the ranch, less the rancher, but with all guns available. With them went the author armed with a measuring tape.

The stiffening carcass of the bear was still in the attitude of its attack, and the distance from the hind paw to the end of the extended

the Peace, and he became convinced that he could develop an oil field there. Thomas also went as far as acquiring a charter for a railway (who did not in those days?), the Pacific, Peace River and Athabasca Railway. Its route from the Pacific was to be via the Nass River valley, the Skeena River valley, and others to the Peace River Gap and into the Prairies as far as Prince Albert. It went the way of most such charters—nowhere.

To make travel easier between his two proposed resource extraction operations, in the winter of 1915-16 Thomas built a large sternwheeler for service on the Peace River. He named it the *front claws in their raised position was fourteen feet. Quite an apparition to meet in the morning when the mind is still partially numbed from sleep! There were no other bears around.*

Some days later the author, accompanied by a professional colleague, visited a bridge site on the new highway from Chetwynd to Hudson Hope that the survey crew was working on. It was early and there had been a shower just after dawn. As we stood by the crossing, which was awaiting the design of the bridge, we were quite alone. Suddenly we both became aware of a large imprint in the soft earth by the river's edge. In size and form it matched exactly the bear paws which we had seen only a few days before.

The retreat to the truck, which was a few hundred feet away, was wordless and as expeditious as possible, very nearly reaching a full run. Both of us looked around several times to see if we were being followed. We were not. That bear had simply gone on its way. Neither of us fully emptied our lungs until the truck doors were closed—then we both burst out laughing.

As an aside to the above, we learn from Herbert Anscomb's diary of an encounter with a bear in this general area about twenty years earlier. Anscomb was B.C.'s minister of Public Works early in the last war, and in a visit to the area his car became mired in the mud between Fort St. John and Hudson Hope. With his companion he walked on ahead for help, until they came upon a young Native girl who had been mauled by a bear. Anscomb insisted on staying beside her while his companion hurried on for assistance. In doing this he placed himself in danger, as that bear might well have returned.

D.A. Thomas, and as well as outfitting the boat to burn coal or wood, he also ensured it was equipped to burn his oil, once it started flowing. Ironically it never ran on coal or oil, its firemen feeding its boiler with cordwood logs. (Cordwood logs are four feet in length. They are named after a cord, which is a measure of such logs, four feet wide by four feet high by eight feet long.)

The *D.A. Thomas* was an excellent boat, 167 feet in length and 40 feet in width, beautifully appointed, and with its twin smokestacks it was distinctive as well as efficient. It distinguished its owner even when the coal find came to nothing—there simply was not enough time to develop it before World War I, and it was not the best area anyway—and when the oil drilling also came up empty. By then it was time for Mr. Thomas to return to the land of his birth.

It was a cruel turn of fate that Thomas came so close, but not close enough. If he had looked about 85 miles south and east of Hudson Hope, at a place to be called Tumbler Ridge near the Murray River, he would have found coal very close to the surface and in sufficient quantity to satisfy a large segment of the Japanese steel industry several decades later. Furthermore, if he had moved to the vicinity of Fort Edmonton rather than Fort Vermilion, to a place to be known as Leduc, he would have found and drilled an oil well productive enough to realize his wildest dreams. In his venture he invested $250,000 and lost most of it.

The *D.A. Thomas* was purchased by the Lamson Hubbard Trading Company, which operated it reasonably profitably until 1922, though they soon realized that it was too big for the area and for the business available. In these years it used only a very small percentage of its 100-passenger and 200-ton freight capacity. In addition to this, when it was loaded it drew five feet, so was regularly getting hung up on sand bars. It sat idle for two years and then was snapped up by the Hudson's Bay Company, which

had a habit of cashing in on the failed dreams of others. They had even less luck in finding business, and in 1927 the *D.A. Thomas* did not make even one trip. In 1930 the HBC decided to move it downstream into the Athabasca-Slave River area. This required running it through the Vermilion Chutes, rapids that had never

The D.A. Thomas *(left) was designed by Vancouver boatbuilder George Askew, built in the winter of 1915-16, and launched at Dunvegan on the Peace River by an English industrialist of similar name, later to become Lord Rhonnda. With its distinctive twin stacks, it was the largest vessel ever on the Peace River—167 feet long by 40 feet wide—and fully loaded with 200 tons of freight it drew five feet. It was reported to have cost $119,000. The boat was fully outfitted for luxury travel, with a large dining saloon, and was reported to have made the 250-mile upstream trip from Peace River town to Hudson Hope in seventeen hours. (Usually the trip took several days with numerous stops.) Unfortunately it was too large, and drew too much water, to be easily operated on the Peace. It was finally acquired by the Hudson's Bay Company. In 1930 the HBC, seeing the writing on the wall for their oversize sternwheeler with the imminent arrival of the Northern Alberta Railway in Dawson Creek, B.C., decided to move the vessel downstream on the Peace to the Athabasca River. In order to do this it had to run the Vermilion Chutes, located about 50 miles beyond Fort Vermilion. The* D.A. Thomas *made it through the Chutes, though with its hull wracked in the process. This might have affected the steering, as the vessel went aground heavily some miles downstream, near Fort Fitzgerald, and was immovable (above). Captain John Cadenhead visited the site of the boat's demise seven years later and said, "There was nothing but a bunch of ribs sticking out of the mud, and the kids playing in the wheelhouse." It remained as shown for some years before the river demolished it.*

Preceded by rapids, the Vermilion Chutes, as can be seen in this photo, were several feet in height. There is no indication what the river level was when this photograph was taken, probably quite low. The Hudson's Bay Company sternwheeler Athabasca River *was winched up through the mile-long Chutes in 1915, presumably without damage, but when the much larger D.A. Thomas* made the trip through, travelling downstream in 1930, the hull was wracked and the sternwheel damaged, probably one reason the boat ran aground some distance downstream and was abandoned.

been traversed going downstream by a vessel of this size. These are the only rapids on the river for 700 miles from its canyon upstream of Hudson Hope until its junction with the Slave River. The hull was deformed in the passage, and the boat came close to losing its paddlewheel. For whatever reason, the vessel grounded on a sand bar farther downstream before it reached Fort Fitzgerald, and there it stayed. That was its last voyage.

The first sternwheeler on the Peace River in British Columbia was the *St. Charles*, a vessel put there by Bishop Emile Grouard who had it built at Dunvegan in 1903. Although a very small boat, it ran the 525-mile trip from Vermilion Chutes to Hudson Hope regularly in service to the Bishop and his flock, and no doubt to others as necessary. Grouard was one of Canada's great frontiersmen, serving the Peace River country for over 70 years following his arrival in 1862.

In 1905 the *St. Charles* received competition, which led to its retirement, when the HBC launched the *Peace River*, a lovely boat,

110 feet in length, that operated very successfully for another ten years. This vessel was replaced by the larger *Athabasca River,* which held sway until 1919, by which time the *D.A. Thomas* was ruling the waters.[5]

After all this, the area returned to its usual unnoticed state, but in its skies another mode of transportation was stirring or, it might be said, trying its wings. A man called Grant McConachie was the creator of Independent Airways (later Yukon-Southern

This picture serves better than words to demonstrate the impotence of the B.C. provincial government regarding that part of the province east of the Rocky Mountains. Taken in September 1917, it shows Premier H.C. Brewster on the Scow de Luxe, *as it was laughingly referred to by other members of the group who travelled on it with Brewster up the Parsnip to the Finlay River and as far as they could get down the Peace before coming to the Peace River Canyon and the Ne Parle Pas rapids. The party included T.D. Pattullo, minister of Lands at that time. Not shown is the Evinrude outboard motor they had. After a hike over the portage, they might well have been met by the luxurious* D.A. Thomas *and proceeded in better style. In 1917 this was the only way that anyone could get to the Peace River Block and stay within B.C. (unless they climbed over the Rockies), and it remained so for another 35 years. A newly elected premier would have been loath to travel through another province to visit all areas of his recently acquired jurisdiction.*

Air Transport), flying first from Charlie Lake (a few miles north of Fort St. John) to Fort Nelson and then out of Edmonton farther north. McConachie, who eventually became the founder and president of Canadian Pacific Air Lines, pressed the national government unceasingly to build airstrips on the way to the far north, and he was a man who usually got what he wanted.[6]

What McConachie achieved became known as the Northwest Staging Route to Alaska, and it brought about Canada-U.S. intergovernmental discussion—and action—concerning airports, culminating in co-operation and cost-sharing during World War II. As the 1930s progressed, airstrips and finally airports appeared at Grande Prairie, Fort St. John, Fort Nelson, Watson Lake, Whitehorse, and Fairbanks in Alaska, a series of stepping-stones for air travel to the north. The significance of this was not evident in the 1930s, but in the decade to follow it became obvious.[7]

However, before going further into that, the 1930s also saw the most remarkable of all the visitations to the part of B.C. east of the Rockies.

The year 1934 was a dreadful one in British Columbia. It was the year the Army took over the province's work camps for the unemployed and also took responsibility for roadbuilding from the Department of Public Works. They paid the unfortunate men in the camps, who were unable to find work in the Great Depression and who would otherwise have starved, 30 cents a day for their labours on such roads as were built.

Two years before this, a man had come to the Peace River area on a hunting trip. Charles Bedaux learned how desperately the residents wanted an overland route to the Pacific Ocean, and in 1934 he returned to the area, accompanied by his wife, her companion and maidservants, a mechanic, a Scottish gamekeeper, a Swiss guide, a Hollywood film crew, and some friends, and announced that he was undertaking a great exploratory trip northwards and westwards as a first step to solving their problem. He let it be known that he would hire many of the locals at the unheard-of wage of four dollars per day, with board, to assist him.

Naturally he was very well received. He had been well received in Alberta as well, and was seen off in Edmonton by the lieutenant-governor. Although Bedaux was a resident of America at that time and a naturalized American citizen, he had been born in France and maintained a chalet there, where he regularly entertained the Prince of Wales. He obviously had lots of money.

It seems the Stikine was his choice for ocean access, as Telegraph Creek was mentioned as the final destination, and the expedition hoped to find a pass in the Rockies north of the Peace

The photo above shows one of the Bedaux expedition vehicles on Cameron Hill. Steel tracks on a grassy slope of 34 degrees to the horizontal do not give good braking, so it was necessary to snub it down with cables. The total descent to the Cameron River was 1150 feet. The Cameron is a major tributary of the Halfway River. Someone has marked this negative for cropping to make the hill look steeper—probably one of the Hollywood film crew who took the picture.

to lead them there. They did find one, but they never went the full distance. Just what this exploration was meant to achieve, especially in view of the economic conditions, was never made clear, but no one really cared. One of the additions to Bedaux's party was a renowned British Columbia surveyor and civil servant, F.C. Swannell, who was put there by a provincial government that obviously wanted to be associated with such a noble venture

This photo shows three of the six vehicles specially manufactured by Citroen and shipped out from France for this expedition. Only five set forth, one no doubt being cannibalized for spares. The half-tracks were excellently suited to the Sahara Desert, where their type had excelled. The large, retractable, steel roller between the narrow-tread front wheels worked well on soft sand when the front wheels sank in, but for B.C. swamps and mudholes it only added weight and made it more difficult to back out. As a result, when the trucks bogged down, which they did regularly, they had to be pulled out by horsepower. They only reached the junction of the Graham and Halfway Rivers, about 80 miles from Fort St. John, in 23 days before Bedaux abandoned them all in spectacular fashion, running three over a cliff and rafting a fourth down the river under a cliff from which he dropped huge rocks on it. All this was duly recorded by the film crew—at least he got some film footage out of it. He left the other two in the bush.

at such an opportune time, whatever it achieved in the long run. Swannell later published an excellent diary of the trip.

Bedaux sent out an advance party on April 30, led by a former Hudson's Bay man turned B.C. land surveyor by the name of Ernest Lamarque. Lamarque had hoped to find a pass at the head

The Westergaard Ranch is located about 70 miles northwest of Fort St. John on the Halfway River. The Westergaard family arrived in the early 1920s from Denmark. Here mother, daughter, and grandchildren are shown in 1934 with Charles Bedaux, who is holding a cabbage in a pot, both probably supplied by the kindly ranch people, who also provided him with pack horses to substitute for the abandoned half-tracks. The man on the left is M. Balourdet, Bedaux's French mechanic. Bedaux came to an unfortunate end. French-born but a naturalized American, he turned up in Vichy, France after the German invasion and was often seen in the company of high-ranking German Army officers. He then obtained a commission from Vichy to investigate building an oil pipeline from inland Africa to Algiers. When the Americans successfully invaded North Africa they apprehended him and shipped him back to the States. On April 30, 1944, just before he was to be indicted for treason, he committed suicide in Miami.

These are the river boats that Charles Bedaux ordered up from McLeod Lake and Summit Lake to transport his party, less horses and horsemen, back to the Peace River portage on his return trip to Fort St. John. They were substantial. One, 45 feet long of 5-foot beam with an eight-horse outboard, regularly made the 350-mile trip from Summit Lake to Whitewater (Fort Ware) under the guidance of Arnold Myers, Fred Fosberg, and Ludwig Smaaslet. Note the movie camera and tripod in the boat in the background.

of the Prophet River but that was not to be, and he went on to the Muskwa River, where he did find a pass that he named after Bedaux. The elevation was reported as close to 4500 feet above sea level. On the way there he cleared out what was called a tractor trail, but it could not have been much more than a bare clearing without bridges due to the time factor. This was to accommodate the five Citroen gasoline-powered half-tracked vehicles that Bedaux imported for the journey. These were similar to the half-tracks he had driven across the Sahara Desert.

The main party of the expedition, 47 in number, set forth from Fort St. John on July 22 with the half-tracks and about 50 pack horses loaded down with tanks filled with gasoline for the vehicles. About 80 miles out, at the Westergaard Ranch on the Halfway River, they abandoned their vehicles, which could deal with the bare-ground Sahara but could not cope with the close-spaced trees, rock ledges, boulders, windfalls, rivers, and swamps of the Rocky Mountain foothills. In reducing materials carried, Bedaux jettisoned survey equipment, rendering Swannell furious. They also dumped the tanks of gasoline and proceeded entirely on horseback, with a total of 130 riding and pack animals.[8]

When Lamarque heard of the demise of the motor vehicles he changed to a horse trail immediately. On the ascent of the Fox River to Sifton Pass he used the trail put there in 1898 by Inspector Moody of the North West Mounted Police. He reportedly sent a message to Bedaux telling him that the going from Sifton Pass onwards was much easier and that he was marking lakes suitable for float planes to deliver feed for the horses, but his message never got through. If it had been received, it is possible the expedition would have gone on over the divide for another 160 miles to the Dease River valley and its public road system. (Grant McConachie could have flown the fodder in. He was operating a Fokker single-engine float plane all that summer out of Takla Lake.) And continuing the speculation, if the Citroen company had shipped its product to Telegraph Creek rather than to Edmonton, the mechanical mules would have been waiting at Dease Lake to shuttle Bedaux and his party out to Telegraph Creek by that pioneer roadway in triumph! Frank Swannell might well have suggested this plan if they had given him enough time to come up with it, but trying to take these tractors across the Rockies just did not make sense.

Instead, after descending from Bedaux Pass to Fort Ware, the main party headed part way up to Sifton Pass, then winter warned them off, along with the lack of horse fodder, and they turned back in late September. This was unfortunate as the worst was behind them. In their descent to the Finlay they had traversed some of the roughest terrain in the northwest as they came down the Kwadacha River valley on the western slope of the Rockies, what is now the Kwadacha Wilderness Park, an area overlooked by the Lloyd George icefield and glacier. Swannell made a first mapping of their route over the pass and had all the expedition members sign it. They covered a total of 416 miles outbound.

A sad aspect of their journey was that many of their horses developed foot rot and had to be put down. The leading members of the party returned to the Peace by riding down the Finlay River in river boats sent up from McLeod Lake. They had some excitement in Deserter's Canyon but it was no worse than Fort George Canyon on the Fraser.[9]

Apart from the mapping, they achieved very little except the expenditure of over $250,000 by Bedaux and, through the circulation of these funds, a much better 1934-35 winter for many of the Depression-ridden Peace River area residents. It is worth noting that the official title of the expedition was "The Bedaux Sub-Arctic (Citroen) Expedition."

The supreme irony is how well Bedaux's return trip must have proven to him what most people in the area knew, or at least suspected: that by far the best route for a railway from Fort St. John to Fort Ware was by way of the Peace River Gap and along the Rocky Mountain Trench beside the Finlay.

The next visitation was the greatest of them all, and it was by the Americans.

Prior to World War II, the Americans had looked seriously at the idea of a road to Alaska through Canada, commissioning studies by American institutions, often connected to American universities, that were authorized and paid for by Congress, as is their custom. One of these commissions went to the Battelle Memorial Institute, which looked at several routes and recommended one about where the Cassiar-Stewart Highway is now. Another route went by way of the Rocky Mountain Trench. Never considered was a route on the eastern side of the Rockies.

These studies were conducted in rather leisurely fashion, and nothing concrete ever came from them. However, in early 1942, when President Franklin Roosevelt authorized an urgent update of these, he did so with the screech of Japanese bombs aimed at his battleships still in his ears. These bombs were being delivered by planes based on aircraft carriers located a few hundred miles from Pearl Harbour, so Roosevelt wanted nothing to do with a

WILD HORSES BESIDE THE HALFWAY RIVER

William Ogilvie, Dominion Land Surveyor, later Commissioner of the Yukon, recounts how in 1893 the Hudson's Bay Company officer at Fort St. John, a Mr. Gunn, told him that the company maintained bands of horses on the prairie year round, and that they could forage for themselves throughout the winter, reaching grass through the snow. Most of the animals were completely wild and unbroken.

In the early 1960s the author was fortunate to make a trip by helicopter up the Halfway River valley, which runs north from the Peace midway between Fort St. John and Hudson Hope. The intention was to locate a new bridge site over the Halfway River for the Pink Mountain Road. It was a clear and bright winter's day with the temperature in the minus 30s, and there had been no snow for several weeks, so the animal tracks were all visible in the light snow cover. We could see that each bull moose and its mate and offspring had their own small area in the river flats in a procession of "moose holdings" separated by about half mile intervals. You could determine their movements over the last two weeks by their tracks in the snow.

Suddenly the engine noise startled a band of about twenty wild horses and they broke into full gallop across the snow beneath us. Their coats were long and sleek, each with a huge mane flying in the wind. It was an unforgettable sight. These were the descendants of the HBC horses, and every year the local ranchers and their cowboys rounded them up in the early summer and drove a selected number overland to Grande Prairie to be sold. When the winter is a hard one, as this one was, they put down hay bales at intervals along the valley, and this band had been feeding from one pile.

The bales had been transported by the helicopter we were in, and the stresses of the operation had sprung the cabin doors, resulting in horrendous drafts of super-cold air. This was bearable while we travelled in the sunlight, but when the early darkness fell as we returned, we nearly froze. The pilot was all right because he had sheepskin-lined pants and knee boots. But it was worth it!

TIMETABLE
OF ALASKA HIGHWAY CONSTRUCTION

1938: First discussion between the U.S. Alaska International Highway Commission and the Canadian B.C./Yukon Highway Committee.

1940: "Very negligible" is the joint opinion vis-a-vis defence.

1941: The Commission and Committee named above met again to discuss air routes.

December 7, 1941: Pearl Harbour.

February 2 and 4, 1942: The assistant chief of the U.S. Army Engineers is asked for a plan. Two days later he is told to go ahead.

February 11, 1942: The U.S. president authorizes the construction of a pioneer road.

March 2, 1942: Massive quantities of materials are despatched to B.C., Yukon, and Alaska, along with troops and other support personnel.

March 17 and 18, 1942: Letters of Agreement signed. U.S. troops start pouring in to Canada.

March 1942: The U.S. Engineer's 35th regiment is ordered to proceed from Fort St. John to Fort Nelson on the winter road and then start building back towards Fort St. John. The 91st and 341st regiments ordered to build north from Fort Nelson and north from Fort St. John.

April 5, 1942: The 35th regiment arrives at Fort Nelson.

April 18, 1942: Various U.S. Engineer regiments arrive in Whitehorse from Skagway. The 18th, 93rd, 340th regiments start building road north and south of Whitehorse. The 97th regiment arrives in Valdez, Alaska, moves on to Big Delta on the Richardson Highway, and starts building south from there. By this time the total troop complement is 394 officers and 10,765 NCOs and enlisted men.

November 20, 1942: A passable road is completed. From now on the U.S. Public Roads Administration (PRA) is in control—with many troops staying on.

February 18, 1943: Explosion in Dawson Creek, B.C. Five dead and 200 injured. Fire destroys the main street.

September 1943: Peak of construction by PRA. A total of 16,000 men and women are at work, with 11,000 pieces of equipment (10,000 troops still there).

1943: 133 bridges built, all 20 feet long or longer.

July 14, 1943: Name changed from Alcan Highway to Alaska Highway.

August 30, 1943: The Peace River Bridge is completed at Taylor Flats. The contractor is J.R. Roebling of Trenton, N.J. (the contractor for the Brooklyn Bridge). DPW Minister Herbert Anscomb represents B.C.

October 1943: Permanent improvements are completed by PRA. U.S. War Department takes over.

April 1, 1946: The Royal Canadian Engineers (RCE) take over the highway from the American Army. Eighteen permanent road camps are established.

Summer 1946: The Haines Highway connection is opened to civilians. Travellers on the Alaska Highway still need RCMP permission to proceed north from Dawson Creek.

April 1, 1964: The Canadian federal department of Public Works takes over from the RCE.

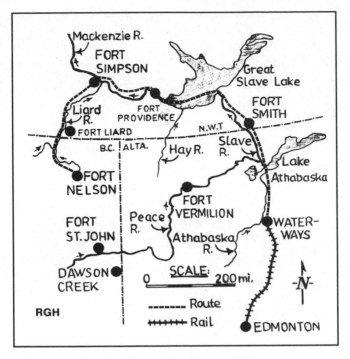

A Long Way Around

route which was within flight range of similar carriers lying off the Pacific coast. For a time the Americans considered a road along the Mackenzie valley, which would be totally safe, but they finally decided that the eastern side of the Rocky Mountains within British Columbia would do just fine. The clincher was the Northwest Staging Route string of airfields, which could easily become coastal defence air bases against the Japanese, especially if they contemplated landings, which at that time seemed quite possible. As well, the airfields would be good back-up facilities to assist in the construction of the road that the president had in mind.[10]

Things happened fast then. On March 18, 1942, the Canadian and U.S. governments issued a joint statement announcing the construction of the Alcan Highway, as it was called. (On July 19, 1943, the name Alcan was dropped in favour of Alaska Highway.) The U.S. Army would make the necessary surveys and construct a pioneer road from Dawson Creek, B.C., to Big Delta, Alaska, a

A LONG WAY AROUND

When the American Army sent two engineer regiments into Fort Nelson in the late spring of 1942 using the winter road then in existence, they must have known that, come the thaw, their only access road would become impassable right through to freeze-up that year. There is no doubt that each unit hauled enough fuel to keep it going for some time, but it could not be enough to keep them supplied all season. The 35th regiment, for example, which worked building the pioneer road to the south, had a vehicle complement of 44 tractors, about half of them diesel powered, and a total of 123 trucks. Working eleven-hour days, six days a week, their fuel consumption was very large. Finding a supply mechanism would determine the success or failure of the operation, and they put their minds to work. It soon became apparent that by the time the southbound operation reached the end of its fuel it would be within few enough miles of Fort St. John to let them drag in extra over the mud, but the unit working north had a real problem.

Difficult problems require imaginative and courageous decisions, and the Army's answer to the problem certainly showed both attributes. They shipped 446 barrels (mostly gasoline, but some diesel) to Waterways, Alberta, by rail, and from there on by what can only be called an odyssey, shown in the adjacent map. From Waterways to Fort Smith the barrels were "portaged," which meant they were carried half the way by water and half by trail. Then they were placed on riverboats on the Slave and shipped down to Great Slave Lake where larger and deeper draught boats were necessary for the 150-mile trip to Fort Providence. Here they were reloaded onto shallow-draught craft for the 500-mile trip down the mighty Mackenzie and up the Liard to Old Fort Nelson, arriving there in August. This route had been used by the residents of Fort Nelson before the war, but only when really necessary.

About eighteen years later the author visited Old Fort Nelson and observed an interesting operation. A semi-trailer flatdeck had been pushed down into the river deep enough for one of a collection of light, shallow-draught barges to lie alongside, and a multitude of brightly painted oil drums were being loaded onto the barge. The destination of the tug and barges there that day was Inuvik. To the obvious question, "Would steel barrels last that many years?" the answer has to be, "Yes, if they were well painted!" [11]

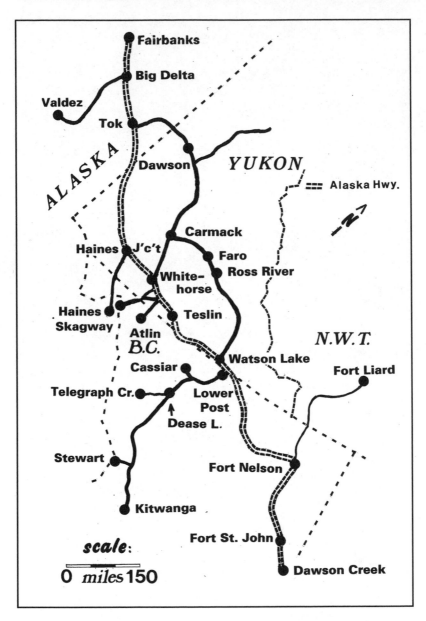

The Alaska Highway and its Offshoots

THE ALASKA HIGHWAY AND ITS OFFSHOOTS

*The Richardson Highway. Prior to World War II this was the primary
highway in Alaska, built in 1923 following the route of a military
telegraph line from Valdez to Fairbanks, through Big Delta. The
Alaska Highway construction started south from Big Delta.*

*The Klondike Highway. This highway, completed in the 1950s, joined
Whitehorse to Dawson City and replaced the legendary winter
trail. In the 1980s it was extended to Tok in what the Americans
called the Taylor Highway, which completes a loop for tourists in
recreational vehicles visiting Dawson en route to Fairbanks.*

*The Dempster Highway. Originating from an intersection a few miles
south of Dawson City, this highway leads through the tundra for
more than 300 miles to the mouth of the Mackenzie River where
it flows into the Arctic Ocean near Inuvik. It is truly a bus ride to
the High Arctic, but a long one. A converted winter ice road, it is
the ward of the federal government and a great boost to the Inuit
people.*

*The Haines Highway. This was built from Haines on the coast to Haines
Junction on the Alaska Highway concurrent with the building of
the Alaska Highway. In the late 1970s the Americans proposed
that it be upgraded to full two-lane rural arterial standard. They
negotiated a joint project for this with the Yukon and British
Columbia governments—the Shakwak Highway Improvement
Agreement.*

*The Atlin Road. Short in mileage (only 65 miles from Atlin to Jake's
Corner on the Alaska Highway), but long on history, this is one of
B.C.'s oldest northern roads, only matched by the Telegraph Creek
to Dease Lake Road.*

*The Robert Campbell Highway. Completed in recent years and made
up of intermittent roads, this highway is named after the original
Hudson's Bay Company trader in the area. It runs from Watson
Lake past Ross River and Faro and ends on the Klondike Highway
at Carmack.*

*The Stewart Highway. Also known as the Cassiar-Stewart Highway,
this 465-mile offshoot is the longest of them all and is fully described
in the text.*

*The Liard Highway. This oil-industry road was built progressively and
finally reached Fort Liard, a settlement that up until then depended
on riverboats, winter trails, or, of course, bush planes. This highway
continues northwards and eastwards.*

settlement about 70 miles south of Fairbanks. Contractors would then complete the road under contract to the U.S. Public Roads Administration. The contracts would be let on a cost-plus basis, and construction would proceed with all possible speed. The U.S. agreed to maintain the highway for the duration of the war and for six months thereafter, unless the Government of Canada preferred to assume earlier responsibility for maintenance of the Canadian section. (Canada did not choose to pursue this option.)[12]

That spring a goodly proportion of the home-based American Army field engineering regiments, complete with their equipment, boarded trains all over the United States. For some their destination was the northern terminus of the Northern Alberta Railway, a small town by the name of Dawson Creek, B.C. Others were despatched from Seattle by sea to Wrangell, Skagway, and Valdez in Alaska (see the map "The Alaska Highway and its Offshoots"). All in all, seven engineering regiments were engaged in the operation totalling 394 officers and 10,765 enlisted men.

By the summer, more and more of the huge resources of the United States of America arrived in Dawson Creek in the way of soldiers, equipment, supplies, and support workers, and the population of the town kept on doubling. When on February 13, 1943, the main business district burned to the ground in an explosion and conflagration that involved some rather poorly protected U.S. Army explosives, with 5 dead and 200 injured, no one looked for scapegoats; they simply rebuilt the streets and went on doubling their numbers![13]

Dawson Creek was not the starting point for the road construction. This commenced from the end of the existing road north of Fort St. John, about 50 miles away and on the far side of the Peace River, which was crossed by a ferry. There the U.S. Army built a magnificent base camp, dubbed Fort Alcan, and at the same time started operations out of Fort St. John airport. These operations included airborne transfers of basic camp facilities for Fort Nelson and Watson Lake, and of course the transfer of supplies and personnel to Fairbanks, Alaska.

A tractor pulls a pull grader that has finished ditching on the pioneer road and is now grading the material across. A patrol grader (self-powered) follows, cleaning up. The 35th Regiment of the U.S. Engineers had six of the pull graders and three patrol graders. They were typical of the equipment the seven engineer regiments had, and with them the Army built the 1400 miles of pioneer road in one season. The pull grader operator's job was not easy. If the blade hit a rock or a strong root it would jerk and react to the wheel in his hands, wrenching his arms and wrists (and sometimes breaking bones). In very dry conditions he was continually immersed in dust.

THE SIX BY SIX BLUES

Found written by an Alcan truck driver on a sign by the pioneer road.

Winding in, or winding out,
There certainly can be no doubt,
That the man who built this road -
Was going to Hell,
Or coming out!

This is the finished pioneer road grade for the Alaska Highway—without gravel, but the clay is well packed down to reduce the dust, making it slippery in the rain. The width appears to be about twelve to fourteen feet, basically one lane requiring that drivers take care when passing approaching traffic. The final roadway width completed by the U.S. Public Roads Administration was 26 feet, with a 22-foot-wide gravelled surface.

As you can see in this photo, the debris of bushes and felled trees was pushed to the side and not burnt. When they widened the road they built debris storage areas alongside the road, separated from the highway by an off-take road of sufficient length to allow them to clear a round area 100 to 150 feet in diameter at the end of it. The debris was piled here. From the air these areas resembled a row of huge commas alongside the road, with the tails of the commas touching the cleared road right-of-way. The original intention was to build the finished highway alongside the pioneer road, but eventually they built most of the final roadway right on top of it.

Before the frost left and the ground softened up that spring, Army bulldozers and other all-terrain vehicles, motor graders, and trucks, with multiple trailers, set forth on the existing winter road, headed for Fort Nelson. Very soon they were there and the camp was completed, and they started northwards, building road towards Watson Lake.[14]

Meanwhile at Watson Lake, personnel, equipment and supplies were arriving via the Stikine River and the road from Telegraph Creek (described in Chapter 4) to build the strip into an airport and to set up a supply depot, and they also started off building road. At Whitehorse troops arrived from Skagway, and from Valdez to Fairbanks, and these troops started building road either southwards or northwards.

It was like a huge military campaign fought on multiple fronts—which indeed it was—and it was fully successful. By the late fall of 1943 a road existed from Dawson Creek, Mile Zero, to Big Delta, Mile 1417. It was not much of a road in places, and at some spots tracked vehicles stood by to haul trucks out of muskeg swamps and frost boils (which are unstable areas of mud lasting from the spring thaw), but it was a road, and the American Army convoys used it.[15]

Muskeg was a curse (almost as bad as the mosquitoes and the no-see-ums), as it was to be later on the Hart Highway construction and had been at Prince Rupert. At the northern end of the highway, mostly north of Watson Lake, the challenge of working with permafrost, permanently frozen soil, was a factor. For example, when a bulldozer started working an area where moss overlaid permafrost in the spring of the year, and if it was on a slope, even a gentle one, the tractor simply started sliding, with the moss rippling up in front of it. It was that moss, and other vegetation, which had kept the ground underneath frozen, and as soon as it was stripped off, the soil turned to soupy mud. Such conditions brought tears of frustration and near despair. They finally learned not to touch the humus on top of the permafrost at all. Instead they piled brush on it, up to seven feet in thickness, and dumped gravel on top. This worked, as the brush and humus insulated the ice-filled soil below.

Through the winter months the temperature remained frigid. The engineer companies had many Black troops in them, mostly from the southern states, and they served their country well that year, in B.C. and Yukon conditions that were quite unknown to them. The American Army as a whole deserved respect and thanks from Canada for the job they did on this venture on very short notice.

Within the year the U.S. Army handed the road over to the Public Roads Administration, the major highway engineering administration of the U.S. government. That organization employed contractors, who went back and widened, graded, and gravelled the pioneer road in the years following (and sometimes built new grade alongside it), and it gradually became a highway. At the peak of construction in September 1943 there were a total of 16,000 men working on the highway, along with 11,000 pieces of equipment.[16]

The specified road grade width of 36 feet was only achieved as far as Mile 75. After that it was reduced to 26 feet, with a two-inch-thick crushed gravel surface of 22 feet width. Under that there was a four- to ten-inch thickness of natural gravel, although in muskeg areas the gravel could be very much thicker. In these places gravel sources were scouted out by plane, quite probably the first time that was ever done. On November 20, 1943, the U.S. declared it had created a passable road to Alaska.[17]

In the beginning, ferries crossed the main rivers and temporary bridging the lesser ones. Now more permanent structures were built, including, among others, bridges crossing the Liard, Muskwa, and Sikanni Chief rivers, and of course the Peace River at Taylor Flats at the south end of the highway. The latter bridge was completed on August 30, 1943.

In 1946, when the war with Japan was over, the Americans handed it all over to the Canadian Army. Before many years passed the federal authorities failed to watch the installation of local

The upper picture shows a large military convoy on the pioneer road in 1943, in the rain and the mud. It must be assumed that the man in the foreground is not going to take a quick dip!

The second picture, below, shows the solution to the first a year later. Lined up on the finished roadway, 26 feet in width, is an almost endless line of pre-war-vintage gravel trucks, put there by the U.S. Public Roads Administration, which finished the road. Pavement would come very much later.

services well enough, and a water main was built too close to the northern cable anchorage of the Peace River Bridge. In that area, even a small amount of water added to a soil slope can be trouble, and when the pipeline settled and cracked, water from it seeped into the ground. The resulting instability in the riverbank caused a slippage that moved one of the anchorages, and the bridge collapsed. This occurred in October 1957, and road traffic was immediately diverted to the new BC Railway Bridge that had recently been constructed nearby. The Canadian government was left with the task of building a new bridge over the Peace River.[18]

At this point it is a good idea to look at the conditions Canada and the United States agreed to in their joint statement of March 18, 1942, as little seems to be known of them. The Canadian Government agreed (a) to provide the right-of-way for the highway; (b) to waive all import duties, sales taxes, and licence fees on equipment and supplies required for its construction; (c) to remit income tax on the income of the U.S. citizens employed in its construction or maintenance, and facilitate their admission to Canada; and (d) to permit the use of timber, gravel, and rock along the route of the highway as required for its construction. At the conclusion of the war, the Canadian part of the highway was to pass to Canadian control, with the stipulation that citizens of the U.S. would not be discriminated against in its subsequent use.[19]

As well, at about this time the Canadian government passed a statute declaring that U.S. troops were subject to American military law rather than Canadian laws while working on the highway, and this was soon extended to U.S. civilians working on the highway. The American military police efficiently and enthusiastically enforced this adjustment to the law of Canada as it applied to civilians and soldiers alike, and the RCMP, instead of resenting this, welcomed it as it assisted them greatly. It must be assumed that unsuspecting travellers entering the highway were informed at the road blocks of their change in status from free citizens to wards of the American Army. (Up until 1951, travellers

The lower photograph shows the completed Alaska Highway near the original community of Fort Nelson. The new settlement, visible in the photograph, that built up around the highway soon pre-empted that name. The roadway has been oiled to hold down the dust. It also shows the telegraph and telephone line to Alaska, built by the Americans. The right-of-way was 300 feet wide, very nice for a highway maintenance authority, but rather too much room to have clear of buildings in a community, especially in the north in the winter. When taverns were eventually built on both sides of the road, customers who had imbibed liberally and were turned out of one would try to cross to the other side. Often they lay down in the snow for a rest part way across, which to the author's knowledge was the last rest for at least two of them. They were found frozen stiff in the morning.

The upper photograph is the temporary low-level bridge across the Sikanni River. It was soon replaced by a higher structure.

northbound from Mile Zero on the Alaska Highway required a permit to do so from the RCMP.)

It is remarkable that even under the threat of immediate air attack, as the Americans were when they negotiated this, they still looked after their interests very well indeed! To this day Canada cannot charge American trucks any fees additional to those paid by Canadian trucks when they travel the Alaska Highway or its connections. One of these connections was a road from Haines, Alaska, near Skagway, to Haines Junction on the highway, and this became a protected route that was not open to civilians until the summer of 1946.

As far as Dawson Creek was concerned, it was a good ride while it lasted, but when the Americans handed the highway over to the Canadian Army, that organization preferred Whitehorse to a headquarters in Dawson Creek. The southern city became Mile Zero in influence as well as in name, with only a small monument to mark its previous status. The loss of the American input also led to a sharp recession in the economy of the whole Peace River area, which lasted for a number of years after the war until oil and gas discoveries brought another boom.

In 1964 the Canadian Army passed the administration and operation of the Alaska Highway to the federal department of Public Works. The department at first operated road maintenance camps as part of itself, but finally, as with most road maintenance operations in B.C., it was privatized. The major depots were at Fort Nelson and Watson Lake, with sixteen intermediate permanent camps.

The Alaska Highway quickly became the main transportation artery, along with air, for B.C. east of the Rockies and for the southern Yukon. The highway developed offshoots, primary among them the Cassiar-Stewart Highway, completed in 1964 and now known as Highway 37. This highway stretches from Kitwanga, a Native village on the Yellowhead Highway 70 miles west of Smithers, to meet the Alaska Highway in B.C. near Watson Lake, a distance of 465 miles (see the map entitled "The Alaska

THE BLACK FENCE

Glaciation, or ice flows, across road surfaces can be a problem in the far north. These ice flows, which are in effect small glaciers, about a foot thick initially and seldom more than twenty feet wide, advance down a gentle slope toward the road surface. They are usually triggered by springs or seepage, and they are helped along by a moderate snowfall, extremely cold temperatures, and many short winter days of bright sunlight. When they cross the road surface and are allowed to develop, they are very difficult to remove and may cause many difficulties later on. The short day's sunlight in the far north in winter, even at temperatures far below freezing, causes minute water flows on the face of the ice, and when the sunlight lessens as darkness approaches, this mobile water refreezes at the toe. In this way the glacier advances. Light snowfall freezes to the ice flow and maintains or adds to its thickness, and to its progress.

These ice flows are not usually a problem for a road that is frequently travelled and is constantly maintained in winter in the fashion of those in the south. They are a problem for roads that count the number of cars passing per week instead of per day, and the number of snowploughing trips per month instead of per week—roads that are nonetheless vital to those who use them. Nowhere was this problem more prevalent than on the Atlin Road. But at some point in time someone had devised, or copied, a very ingenious yet simple solution.

The answer was to build a small fence at the edge of the road on its upper side. The fence consisted of light wooden posts a few feet apart, with black tar paper, one roll width high, stapled to the posts. The paper's lower edge touched the ground.

When the leading edge of the ice came within an inch or so of the paper in its progress downhill, the water flowed under the black paper as the sun shone. When the mobile water started to freeze as the sunlight waned, the retained heat of the sun in the black paper stopped the freezing process—but only for an inch or two back. Beyond that distance the re-freezing occurred on the glacier. In effect, the ice layered itself, with its leading edge vertical and rising up behind the black paper. As the winter progressed, this was almost a magical process to observe, and if the ice threatened to overtop the paper, simply adding height of paper was the answer.

The laws of Nature were turned against it, and the effects of sun and shadow were used to help road maintenance rather than to hinder it.

(Author's Note: The highly scientific theory advanced above is entirely the author's. If the reader does not believe it, he or she is fully entitled to think up another! All the author knows for certain, from his experience in the field, is that the black fences worked, with the result described.).

Highway and its Offshoots"). Its major strategic advantage is that it is an alternative routing, though a distant one, for much of the Alaska Highway should that be needed.[20]

The original highway project was intended to connect Cassiar, the asbestos mining centre of B.C., with an overseas shipping point inside the province, for which the provincial government chose Stewart, a small mining town at the head of Portland Canal. The provincial government built the road, and the company dutifully hauled its entire product the full length of it and hauled diesel and heating oil back to its plant. Both ends of this road were then connected to the overall highway system, the north end to the Alaska Highway and the south end to the Yellowhead Highway.[21]

The rationale for this huge expenditure of provincial funds, if there was one, was presumably to develop the area and the port. Any return from the haulage operation was far less than the maintenance cost of the highway. If this highway had not been built, both the output of the mine and the oil supplies would have moved as they had previously, via the Alaska Highway and the White Pass and Yukon Railway.

What the highway did do was assure the demise of the historic railway, which found that it could not continue without the asbestos haul (and other revenue). However, it did reopen later, as a summer service to the tourists who came on the cruise ships that in later years found Alaska to be a lucrative destination. The Victoria-based politicians did not foresee that asbestos would become an unacceptable product, which closed the mine and idled a great number of trucks not many years after they commenced their marathon road trip.

The highway is maintained out of a number of road camps, the main one at Good Hope Lake at the northern end close to the Cassiar junction. The others are located at Meziadin Lake, Bob Quinn Lake, and Dease Lake.

The next offshoot in order of importance was the Klondike Highway from Whitehorse to Dawson City, which took the place of the historic winter trail along the Yukon River. (A road from

The Peace River Bridge was not the only suspension bridge erected by the Americans on the Alaska Highway. The Liard River Bridge at Mile 496 was the other of that construction. It was of a temporary design, as the Bailey bridging used for the stiffening truss was never intended to be permanent—unfortunately the Peace River Bridge did not turn out to be permanent either!

Whitehorse to Carmack predated the Alaska Highway.) This 300-mile-long link was completed in 1949 and is currently paved throughout, although not with a permanent-type pavement. In the 1980s the State of Alaska, in co-operation with the Yukon government, built a second connection from Dawson City back to the Alaska Highway, rejoining it near a hamlet called Tok. This road, the Taylor Highway, allows the American tourists, who in recent years have been flocking into the area in their recreational vehicles, to circle around through Dawson City on their way to or from Fairbanks. They mostly come by the Alaska State Ferry to Haines and up the Haines Highway, or by the ferry to Prince Rupert and up the Cassiar-Stewart Highway. Others make the long overland trip, as the U.S. Army did in 1942.

In the late 1970s the Americans signed an agreement with British Columbia and the Yukon to upgrade the Haines Highway to full two-lane standard and to repave it. This project included an improvement to the Alaska Highway from Haines Junction through to the highway's entrance to Alaska. This was called the Shakwak Highway Project. The majority of the cost was borne by the U.S., and it is unlikely that such friendly co-operation between jurisdictions has been matched anywhere else in the world.[22]

More recently the Robert Campbell Highway has been built from Watson Lake to Ross River and Faro, meeting the Klondike Highway at Carmack. And finally there is the Dempster Highway, the longest of all the offshoots, a road on which you can go by bus to the start of the high Arctic—a two-day trip that quite often takes longer.

All in all it is a wonderful transportation jigsaw puzzle finally put together, with rail, road, river, and air all playing their part—and immensely helped along by a world war.[23]

Immediately after the war, work finally got under way to build the long-desired highway to link the Peace River area with the rest of British Columbia through the Rocky Mountains. In the first two years, 210 miles of the 250 between Prince George and Dawson Creek were let to contract using a route through Pine Pass and following the Pine River eastwards. This took place under the administration of Premier John Hart of the wartime coalition government, and it was named the Hart Highway for him. Hart was no doubt inspired by reports of the difficulty which Public Works Minister Herbert Anscomb had in visiting the Peace River area during the war. Anscomb had driven through the States and Alberta to reach this remote corner of his jurisdiction—he obviously did not favour riverboats and a twelve-mile portage. Anscomb represented British Columbia at the opening of the first Peace River Bridge in August 1943, when he accepted the bridge on behalf of the province.

In the building of this highway the province courageously proposed to leave behind the cost-plus contracting measures previously used on most undertakings of this size, and the work was competitively tendered, primarily in two very large contracts.

TIMETABLE OF THE
PACIFIC GREAT EASTERN RAILWAY
(subsequently the British Columbia Railway)

1912: Premier Richard McBride proposes a new railway linking Vancouver with Fort George (subsequently Prince George).

October 1913: First spike driven on the North Shore line. Service started the next summer between North Vancouver and Whytecliff, 12 miles. This line ran until 1928, when it went out of service.

1916: Service started between Squamish and Clinton.

1929: A twice weekly run was in effect from Squamish to Quesnel. No construction beyond Quesnel because of the difficulty of crossing Cottonwood River.

1947: Switched from steam to diesel.

September 11, 1952: First train into Prince George from Quesnel.

1956: Last 40 miles from Squamish to North Vancouver completed.

1958: Line opened from Prince George to Chetwynd, and from there lines finished to Fort St. John and to Dawson Creek.

1971: Line opened from Fort St. John to Fort Nelson.

1990: Total length of track 1387 miles.

Poor access conditions and immediate post-wartime inflation caused one of the successful bidders, an eastern Canadian firm that had worked for the Public Roads Administration on the Alaska Highway, to forfeit its contract when it failed to meet performance requirements. The province ended up contracting the work to a consortium involving the second contractor, an Alberta firm. This was unfortunate, but it was good experience for the provincial government, which successfully tendered the Hope-Princeton work to other ex-Alaska Highway contractors shortly afterwards. The Hart Highway was opened on July 1, 1952.

Not really necessary, but there anyway, is the railway link from the south to the part of B.C. east of the Rockies. The British Columbia Railway runs from North Vancouver to Prince George and on to Dawson Creek, with a branch line from Chetwynd to Fort St. John, and another from there north to Fort Nelson. The butt of jokes for many years because of its sporadic construction, this totally provincial railway, originally named the Pacific Great Eastern, was first built from Squamish, at the head of Howe Sound, to Quesnel, where it stopped for a while on its way to Prince George. This pause ended up lasting for nearly forty years. Squamish also lacked its connection south for many years, but that centre was finally linked to North Vancouver. (The abortive exploratory line that was built running westwards from Prince George is described in Chapter 1.)

Probably the only amusing feature of this sad chapter in B.C.'s transportation history was the initials of the railway's first name. PGE fitted beautifully with "Prince George eventually" or "Please go easy," both of which were well memorized by Premier John Oliver. With his accession to power he became the unwilling inheritor of the railway and its debts from Premier Richard McBride. That "railroad premier" of British Columbia made the mistake of starting it in the first place, something for which his successor never forgave him.[24]

Oliver and those following never got it farther than Quesnel. Then W.A.C. Bennett took up the baton and finished the relay, only to leave his son, Premier Bill Bennett, the aggravation of a royal commission investigating why the Fort Nelson line started out with an $80 million price tag, but finally cost $235 million. The younger premier also had to explain why, when faced with ground difficulties similar to those experienced by builders of the Alaska Highway on its way to Fort Nelson, the railway was built on sheets of plywood at one point. The plywood sheets were supposed to float it over the mud—they did not.[25]

This railway did not bother the highway system. It followed the route of the gold miners alongside Anderson and Seton lakes, but no provincial road remained there to offer competition. On the Interior plateau, and through the Pine Pass, the terrain was kindly and each avoided the other.

And why did it take so long for rail to come to this corner of the province, when in all other areas it preceded, and often stymied, the building of roads? The Peace River residents certainly enjoyed the best of river transportation for a few years with little competition from roads, and none from rail, but the climate killed any profit taken on the water. Continental-style weather behind the Rockies and northern temperatures seldom left more than five months ice-free on the river, sometimes much less than that. When winter roads thawed and broke up in the spring, river transport could not take over, as that was the most hazardous time on the Peace River with ice breakup, debris flow, and snow-melt flooding.

D.A. Thomas soon learned that the people of the northern prairies desired a rail outlet to the Pacific, even as the GTP was building in 1913 from Yellowhead Pass to Prince Rupert. That is why he obtained a charter for his Pacific, Peace River and Athabasca Railway. But World War I killed that. Then in the boom time after that war, in 1928, when settlers were pouring into the Peace River Block, the air was electric with the planning and surveying of the GTP's transcontinental competitors, searching for a good line from Finlay Forks to Stewart across what they called the mineral belt. The Great Depression killed that. The waves from these plans induced Charles Bedaux to plan his great expedition in 1932. He must have realized, when he got underway in 1934, that the depth of the worldwide depression by that time made reconnaissance for a railway a lost cause, but he went ahead anyway.

These two Peace River promoters at least achieved something tangible for their efforts. Thomas built his boat and Bedaux returned with a map of the alpine area that eventually became the Kwadacha Provincial Wilderness Park. In this they did better than one of their kind who came on the scene some decades later, when the Peace River power development was in its early stages. Axel Wenner-Gren was a multi-millionaire from Sweden, and he achieved nothing tangible on the ground, but lots of rumours in the air. He intrigued everyone with a proposal to construct a monorail up the Rocky Mountain Trench to the Yukon—it seems there was nothing that the promoters of the Peace River area were not prepared to take on, at least verbally! Why he would build such a thing along the two huge valleys that he proposed to flood for a reservoir is hard to understand. It was in no way suitable for hauling logs, which would be the output of the area thereafter. The monorail went the way of its double-railed cousins, which is nowhere at all. Wenner-Gren shared the wartime sympathies of Charles Bedaux, not supportive of the Allies, but, unlike Bedaux, he survived them. To his credit, he did create the Wenner-Gren B.C. Development Company, which promptly carried out a $5-million study of the hydro-electric potential of the Peace River for the B.C. Government, which led to the building of the dam, but not by Wenner-Gren.[26]

Truth is indeed stranger than fiction when applied to these unusual individuals—Thomas, Bedaux, and Wenner-Gren—and also, of course, when applied to the American Army and its remarkable incursion into B.C.[27]

What it all proved was that it was not opposition from other modes of transportation that killed a rail line across northern B.C. in the first third of the twentieth century; it was World War I and the Great Depression. World War II brought a magnificent highway—but to the north, not the west!

It will always be debatable whether the Northern Alberta Railway (NAR) would have crossed the Peace River to Fort St. John and farther north if that area had been in Alberta—probably not. Certainly the policies of the Canadian government, estranging the area from B.C. by taking over administration of the Peace River Block, held back the Block's development in the earlier years, when railways were following expanding settlement, but only if the provincial level of government supported them.

The Peace River Bridge at Hudson Hope is the only suspension bridge in British Columbia built with reinforced concrete deck structure and stiffening. It was completed in 1965. As the river was too wild to permit falsework or barges, the concrete roadway sections were swung out to the centre of the channel on the hangers, like transferring trapeze artists. The bridge replaced a reaction ferry, the head ferryman of which distinguished himself by stopping Premier W.A.C. Bennett's limousine-borne entourage when they sought to board first. There was a carload from a nearby Native village, which had been there before them.

The river is flowing away from the viewer, and the road on the right side goes to Chetwynd.

When the NAR arrived in Dawson Creek in 1931, the first thing built was a road to the Peace River, and freight and supplies coming from outside arrived that way, conveyed to the settlements along the river by smaller boats instead of upriver by sternwheeler. The coming of the NAR was of course the reason why the Hudson's Bay Company tried to move the *D.A. Thomas* down to the Athabasca in 1930. River craft, later on mostly diesel tugs and barges, were active on the Peace River in Alberta until well into the 1950s, but the placid days of the sternwheelers were over on that stretch of river.[28]

Shortage of time forbade the consideration of a rail line northwards in the wartime emergency. The only action on rail was a 500-mile railway survey from Prince George to Lower Post by the Parsnip and Finlay valleys, thrown in by Canada and the U.S. as a sop to the locals who were demanding that their city be on a route north. This survey, carried out by the U.S. Army Engineers, took place throughout 1942, cost $2 million, and came to nothing—road surely won out over rail in this.

In the end, despite all the transportation links established— road and rail and finally an excellent air service—and despite the greatest project of them all, the W.A.C. Bennett Dam and the roads and bridges giving access to it, the Ear still turns more readily to the east, as it did in the past and, probably, as it always will!

Finally, in the Truth is Stranger than Fiction Department: Some readers might wonder about Charles Bedaux's forfeiture of these five brand-new Citroen half-tracks to an environment for which they were so completely unsuited and ask, "How did he acquire his great wealth, in view of such a lack of common sense?" The answer is that he earned his money by promoting and selling the first management systems to American factory managers. In other words, he was an efficiency expert![29]

The final irony about these half-tracks is that it was the fully-tracked vehicles—the bulldozers and tracked loaders and shovels, as well as the four-wheel-drive power graders and trucks, that enabled the American Army to build that road so quickly. If any single private agency were to be commended in the building of the Alaska Highway, it might well be the Caterpillar Tractor Company.

Chapter 4

Stikine Country, Cassiar, Atlin, and Teslin, and the Excitement of the Klondike

Transportation poker-playing is triggered by gold strikes, but the promised railways are never built

The northwest corner of British Columbia is another area that experienced periodic visitations from the south rather than a steady growth. It was originally developed—to the extent that it was developed—by the search for gold. There is one notable road in the area, that from Glenora to Dease Lake, but the introduction of the sternwheelers to the Stikine River and Dease, Teslin, and Atlin lakes, as well as the promise of two railways (neither of which was built) led mostly to trailbuilding. The responsibilities of the road authority were no less onerous for that. In 1903 the total length of trails in British Columbia amounted to 4600 miles, which was more than 70 percent of the mileage of roads.[1]

Trails in British Columbia differed from the original "waggon roads" mainly by their width. The Royal Engineers built the best of the trails—also called "mule roads." They specified a minimum width of 4 feet, with 18 inches in the centre "finished smooth and hard with gravel, clay or small stones."[2] In wet areas they were to be "corduroyed"—close laid with logs (see the photo on page 81). This was done to a minimum width of ten feet. The dominion government built its telegraph trails 4 feet wide. George Landvoigt, the first road superintendent at Hope, specified that cattle trails (i.e., that from Hope to Nicola) must be a minimum of 6 feet wide, "as otherwise the cattle, when crowded, will destroy

The Gertrude, *in this 1884 view of Telegraph Creek from the river, has classic lines and a high prow, good to battle the strong current of the Stikine River. The deep cleft in the mountains is the creek valley itself, along which the Collins Telegraph Company men who named it hoped to run their telegraph line up to the Stikine Plateau and on to Atlin. Their project collapsed before they could do so.*

the outer edge." Wagon roads were at first a minimum of 11 feet wide—except that the province said early on that they could be 9 feet wide in the Kootenays! The Cariboo Road was built 18 to 22 feet wide except in the Fraser and Thompson canyons.

It is estimated that at least half of the travelled trail mileage was in the northern half of the province, and a large proportion of that figure was made up by three trail systems: Telegraph Creek south to Hazelton; Telegraph Creek to Teslin; and Telegraph to Dease Lake/Cassiar. Obviously the hub was Telegraph Creek (see map "Trails To and From Telegraph Creek").

Up in this remote corner of the province we encounter five men who featured in the companion volume: William Moore and John Irving, steamboat captains from the Fraser; William Mackenzie and Donald Mann, railway promoters; and Michael Haney, railroad foreman for Andrew Onderdonk when he was building the Fraser Canyon stretch of the CPR. William Moore in particular played an important role in northern gold rushes, including the Klondike.

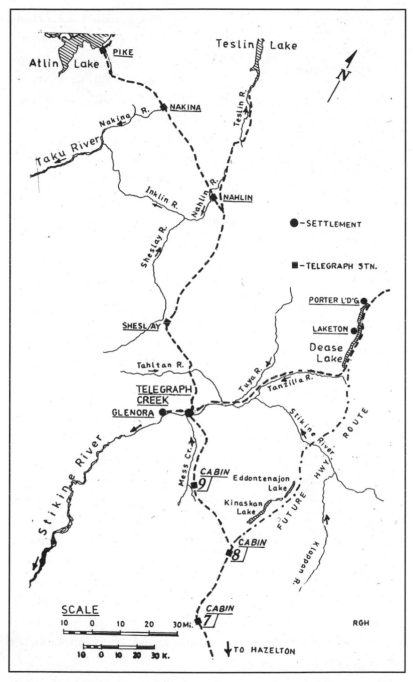

Trails to and from Telegraph Creek

John Irving was 18 years old when he inherited the Victoria Steam Navigation Company from his father in 1872. Eleven years later he created the Canadian Pacific Navigation Company, which ran successfully up and down the coast until he sold it to the CPR, to become its B.C. Coast Service.

While the Collins Overland Telegraph put the spotlight on the area north of the Skeena, it was two prospectors approaching from the hinterland, Thibert and McCulloch, early in 1873, who found the first gold near the source of the Stikine. It was in a stream, soon named Thibert Creek, flowing into the north end of Dease Lake. Captain William Moore immediately heard of it, although it did not become public knowledge until late fall. He went up the Stikine that spring by sternwheeler and struck off on foot across the rough country around the canyon of the Stikine. He panned all the creeks flowing into Dease Lake and found more gold on Dease Creek midway along its length. After he made his find he came down to Victoria and talked the Department of Lands and Works into giving him a contract to build a trail from the head of navigation on the Stikine to the north end of Dease Lake. This, and the transporting of supplies to the gold rush he helped start, made him the most money he had accumulated up until then and put him prominently back into the sternwheeling business after a lapse during which he was close to bankruptcy.[3]

(William Moore was an unbelievable individual. During this "lapse" he organized a 26-mule pack train in 1871 to supply the Omineca gold rush from Hazelton. Then he obtained a supply contract with the Hudson's Bay Company in Hazelton, built two scows at Port Essington with the help of his three sons, and after recruiting about 40 local Natives to help him he rowed, poled, and rope-hauled the fully laden scows up the Skeena.[4] He was a part of every gold rush in B.C. from the Queen Charlottes in 1852 to his death in 1909.)

The trail through from Glenora to Dease Lake eventually became a road, if originally it could be called that. There were many complaints that Moore did a poor job of trailbuilding, and even more about the job done by the roadbuilders who followed him much later. The point he started from on the Stikine River's right bank was twelve miles downstream of the future site of Telegraph Creek village, and the name of the hamlet that sprang up there was a combination of the Scottish and Spanish words for valley and gold—Glenora.

Captain William Moore delivered mail by dog team over 600 miles of Yukon wilderness when he was 74. The man was indestructible.

Glenora, 1899. All that remained here several decades later was a lock-up building put there by the B.C. Provincial Police to hold prisoners until the boat arrived.

This C.E. Fripp rendering of snowdrifts on the Stikine River depicts the challenges of mid-winter travel for B.C.'s northern frontiersmen.

Glenora was in fact a better river port than Telegraph Creek, as it was usable for a longer period in times of low water. The irony was that it was not Captain Moore who built the *Glenora* to serve the 1873 gold rush, but his competitor John Irving. Irving, in his usual wheeling and dealing way, soon sold it, and the word is that he sold it to Moore. In any case, after a relatively short period the *Glenora* came back down to the lower Fraser River.[5] At the upper end of the trail there was a small steamboat put in service named the *Lady of the Lake.*[6] There is also a report that in 1886 Moore built the 80-foot-long *Alaskan* in Seattle and contracted a haul of supplies to Telegraph Creek lasting for four months at $80 per ton out of Fort Wrangell.

All of these transportation developments put the Stikine on the map, and it served as an access route until Dease Creek, Thibert Creek, and McDame Creek lost their lustre. The finds around Dease Lake were quite enough to populate the area with goldseekers for at least a decade, and the inevitable towns came into being and then died, with only scattered remains in the bush to mark their passage. Laketon was one, located midway along the west side of Dease Lake; Porter Landing, at the north end of the lake, is the only one still shown on the maps.[7]

But soon the greatest gold rush of them all started up on the Klondike River, and this had multiple ramifications for the steamboat fraternity, the railway fraternity, and the road fraternity in British Columbia, particularly for the CPR Lake and River Service. The Klondike rush also of course involved William Moore.

Before going further with this, however, we must backtrack a little and examine the series of proposals for rail lines and other means of transportation in this part of the world in this unfolding drama. It is hardly an exaggeration to say that in the last ten years of the nineteenth century, in the coastal areas of northern British Columbia and the Yukon Territory, the events of overland and over-water transportation had all the elements of a Gilbert and Sullivan comic opera, or at the very least a game of musical chairs. They were years full of drama, but always with a background of the ridiculous.

The word ridiculous often describes the antics of the transplanted Englishmen who frequented the province in the last years of the nineteenth century, and it was no different in the land north of the Stikine. The first moves in the poker game of building railways here (and there were to be four hands played) were by the upper crust of the English immigrants, not the run-of-the mill remittance men but the big-game hunters.

Two of these adventurers of the great lone land stand out. Warburton Pike, who started his hunting expeditions in British Columbia in 1889 (the year before his nearly fatal trip to the Peace River Country) and continued them well into the next decade, was one, and with him was a man whose name alone would have endeared him to Gilbert—Sir Edward Clive Oldnall Long Phillipps-Wolley. Sir Edward, a man of wealth before he came to North America, settled down in Victoria after two hunting trips, and Pike, whose nickname was Pikey, started off with real-

The Honourable John Herbert Turner was premier of British Columbia from March 1895 to August 1898, being one of a group of premiers who fell into and out of office in British Columbia at the whim of their enemies, and friends, at the end of the nineteenth century, before they brought in the party system to rationalize things. Turner joined his predecessors and successors in the pursuit and courting of railway promoters and lavished them with land, one reason for his downfall.

estate dealings in the Gulf Islands, where he acquired a lucrative sandstone quarry, and then used this income to finance his numerous expeditions around the province and north of it.[8]

Both of these men became published authors, writing books based on their travels and, as Phillipps-Wolley said, "their enjoyments of barbarism," which included the slaughter of such magnificent animals as musk oxen. Pike wandered the northern latitudes in quest of game, and in one of his trips he went by way of the Cassiar Mountains and the Dease River area, the site of the 1873 gold rush. While there he acquired a gold mine.

He soon brought Phillipps-Wolley into partnership, and together they approached Premier John Herbert Turner for a charter for what they called the Cassiar Central Railway. Turner was pleased to oblige, and he threw in a land grant for 700,000 acres.[9] Their chosen route was from Telegraph Creek due north to Dease Lake, following in the footsteps of William Moore.

Unfortunately the Grand Canyon of the Stikine intruded on this line, along with the high ground and the steep-sided valleys to the north and west of it, and the building of a railway to Dease Lake from Telegraph Creek proved to be quite impossible. The CCR never left the drawing table, but the land grant held good

Sir William Mackenzie was a successful mountain contractor for the first building of the CPR. Along with Donald Mann, his eventual partner, he used his ability with figures to go on to further triumphs, both in railway building and managing and in the promotion, without final building, of railways that remained for all time on the drawing board. Their finest moment came in the building of the Canadian Northern Railway into Montreal, dramatically ending in a tunnel. Their railroad spread across Canada, ending up with a line from Yellowhead Pass to Vancouver.

Sir Donald Mann was the fast talker of the partnership between himself and Mackenzie. His ability for verbal persuasion first set up the politician for a railway charter accompanied by a land grant. Then Mackenzie arranged the financial participation of the particular government, municipal, provincial, or national. This led to a wonderful burst of railway madness in Canada that flourished from the last decade of the nineteenth century to the start of World War I, which put it all to rest.

and the hunters went on to other things, funded by their good fortune. Phillipps-Wolley started a newspaper in Nelson, and for a while he was the editor of the *Vancouver Province*. He also bought Piers Island at the northwest end of the Saanich Peninsula. Pike, as well as building a hotel at Georgina Point on Mayne Island, became a hunting partner to Theodore Roosevelt.

Turner was a bit put out, but soon the whole aspect of the game changed with word of the massive Klondike gold findings in the summer of 1897. The poker game for the right to build a railway to the far northwest corner of Canada really got under way. Next at the table were the two railway promoters par excellence, William Mackenzie and Donald Mann.

They quickly convinced Premier Turner that using the tiresome 100-mile stretch of the Stikine River from Alaskan coastal waters to Telegraph Creek, an icebound, debris-ridden nightmare at times, was not advisable. Much better to come in by an inlet that was more easily travelled and was Canadian all the way—or at least half-Canadian, as the border ran down the centre. This was Portland Canal, and it led to where Stewart lies today. Going by this route would add 180 miles to the trip from Teslin Lake to the coast and involve a crossing of the Stikine River at Telegraph Creek, either by bridge or train ferry, but nonetheless Turner went for it.

Having learned the hard way with Pike and Phillipps-Wolley that actual construction must be assured, Turner ordered an immediate start to the work (an election was fast approaching). They had 20 miles of grade built up the Bear River valley out of Stewart before anyone thought to check further into whether or not their way through the Coast Mountains was feasible by Bear Pass. There they discovered the Bear Glacier, 35 miles from Stewart and firmly in place across the pass, blocking any chance of railway building. There and then the project collapsed. Following these two totally disastrous plays Premier Turner left the game, and he very soon left office, rejected by an electorate that could swallow a lot, but not quite that much.[10]

The Honourable Edgar Dewdney (1835-1916) was the foremost surveyor and builder of trails in British Columbia in its colonial days. After building his masterpiece, the Dewdney Trail, he settled in the Cariboo and surveyed and contributed to the construction of trails in the area, including those from Hazelton and Fort St. James to the Omineca gold finds, before an entry into politics changed his life. Elected to the legislative council in 1868 and 1870, he partook in the Confederation Debate and became a Member of Parliament in 1874, serving for many years in the Canadian House of Commons. He was Indian Commissioner for Manitoba and the Northwest Territories and the Lieutenant-Governor of the Territories before becoming the Lieutenant-Governor of B.C. in 1892. A few days after retiring from that post in 1897 he became part of a transportation venture to the Klondike via the Stikine Trail, and this financially disastrous undertaking is probably what led to him finishing out his life as a mining shares trader in Victoria.

DEWDNEY BACKS THE WRONG TRAIL

The Honourable Edgar Dewdney retired from the position of Lieutenant-Governor of British Columbia on November 30, 1897, after a distinguished career as a public servant at the highest levels. He was 63 years of age. Eleven days later he had a new job, but his private sector employment turned out to be a complete reversal of his success as a public official.

December 11, 1897, was the day when the Klondyke Mining, Trading, and Transportation Company of London, England, announced that it was setting up for business in Victoria, B.C., with Edgar Dewdney as the man in charge of transportation and trading. The company, with a capitalization of 250,000 English pounds, had been created by Sir Charles Tupper, the erstwhile Minister of Railways for Canada, and then High Commissioner in London. Tupper, after a few weeks as Prime Minister in 1896, had returned to London to become a financier in the British capital.

The KMT&T Company immediately advertised widely on the West Coast and in England that it would transport any Klondike goldseeker from Victoria to Dawson City, Yukon, for the sum of $500—and had the proposal worked smoothly, which it did not, it would have been a bargain. The initial operation, the owners said, would be by steamer to the mouth of the Stikine River in winter—the frozen river surface would then be available as a way of travel for two-horse sleighs as far as Glenora. From that point the horse-drawn vehicles would continue by means of a snow road to Teslin Lake. This road was to be kept open by a strong force of horse teams dragging snowploughs. Finally, after a wait there pending the spring breakup, the journey would continue by riverboat to Dawson City. It was an ambitious and courageous proposal.

Eighty teams of horses, a lesser number of sleighs, and three teams of dogs would undertake the initial expedition, as reported by the Victoria Colonist. The trip by sea would be on the Amur, a vessel the company had brought out to the Pacific coast that year from Britain specifically for this use. It was a single-screw, two-masted, steel vessel of 907 tons, 216 feet in length, built in Sunderland, England, in 1890, and in time it was to become a much-loved member of B.C.'s fleet of coastal vessels.

Things did not go quite as planned. How many clients came to ride along with the 80 teams was never made known, but a lack of patronage may well have contributed to the delays that took place, with the Amur finally leaving Victoria on March 3, 1898, complete with Edgar Dewdney. The travellers broke up into two parties at Fort Wrangell; one of the two groups was reported to have only three paying clients in it. Dewdney did not go any farther than that point. He must have become aware of the sad state of the Teslin Trail and decided that it was no place for a recently chairbound 63 year old. Also, it was not the time of year in which to travel an ice trail and a snow road in that country.

For an-on-the spot report we are indebted to a fellow traveller on the trail, John Smith, whose diary was published under the title "Record of a Trip to Dawson, 1898" in the January-April 1952 issue of the B.C. Historical Quarterly. In his entry for April 6, 1898, when he was leaving Telegraph Creek, Smith reports:

We were a few minutes too late in getting off, as we were just behind the Dewdney outfit, who had about eight or ten horses and sleighs and were also taking three passengers, one of whom is Mr. Fripps the artist. Their horses did not keep to the trail very well, and were continually slipping off the frozen crust and getting down into the deep snow, so that we were held up for two or three hours behind them. If either horse or man goes one foot off the trail he is instantly floundering in four feet of wet snow.

Smith's diary is filled with reports of horse teams breaking through the ice on the Stikine, and one team and fully loaded sleigh even went over a 30-foot-high bank on the snow road—without injuries to anyone as it landed in deep snow. Considering the ice trail up the Stikine was 137 miles in length, and the overland route to Teslin Lake 120 miles more, this expedition was no picnic.

Smith met Charles E. Fripp at camp in Telegraph Creek and they struck up a friendship. Fripp was with Dewdney's party and was a sketch artist and correspondent for the weekly London Graphic. He told Smith that he was not reporting favourably on the Teslin route, and his editor later advised his readers that the 1898 expedition to Dawson City by the Stikine was a failure.

Later that year the whole Stikine route bubble collapsed when the Canadian Senate cancelled plans for a rail line (reportedly after a delegation of Yukon miners arrived in Ottawa and convinced a majority of the senators that as the Stikine River was closed by ice for half the year, any railway connecting to river traffic on it was a mistake). Smith reported that he followed Mackenzie and Mann's railway outfit, as he called it, up the Stikine on March 27, and two of their teams went through the ice. One group was carrying the parts for a steamer, and it got through. They set up a large tent at Glenora and filled it with supplies, denied to all but them. Smith says, "They were not admired."

The KMT&T Company made no more trips up the Stikine. The Amur was sold in 1900 and came to the Canadian Pacific Navigation Company soon after. It gave wonderful service up and down the coast, even though it was known as the ugliest ship in the fleet. After another change of ownership it went out of service in 1929.

How much money Edgar Dewdney lost in his support of the wrong trail is not known, but probably this financial reverse led him to accept the assignment to survey the Cascades for a railway route when Premier Dunsmuir offered it in 1901.

The play was far from over however, and Mackenzie and Mann were soon back at the table. This time they had a backer with endless cash for the kitty, the Canadian government. One cut of the cards, one deal to the new player, and it seemed that the game was over. The route this time was by the Stikine. Mackenzie and Mann could change their coats very quickly!

The idea for this route came when an engineer named Duchesnay, a superintendent for the CPR, retraced Moore's Stikine River entry and then struck out to the north and west, heading for the far upper-left-hand corner of the province, to find an "all-Canadian" route to the Klondike. Although the first twenty miles of the Stikine River from tidewater inland were in Alaska, the staunchly Canadian pioneers of that time believed that the terms of the 1846 treaty with the United States regarding free passage removed any problems with this, and they claimed that a route by the Stikine was as good as all-Canadian.

The reason for Duchesnay's trip was that the Canadian transportation giant for which he worked was concerned that practically all the freight and passenger movement to the wonderful new goldfield was by way of Seattle, and it wished in some way to change this. In 1897, after a trip through the area, Duchesnay made one of the most dubious predictions in northern transportation history. He reported that there would be no serious problems in building a wagon road or a narrow-gauge railway across the Yukon Plateau from Telegraph Creek to Teslin Lake, a distance of 145 miles.[11] Teslin Lake was the start of a navigable route to the Yukon River via Teslin River.

He also predicted that this great new route to the Klondike would easily be served by sternwheelers running up the Stikine River. Considering the state of mind of the population of the province in the latter part of 1897, particularly the intense desire of thousands of them to get to the Klondike by hook or by crook, this statement really put the fox in the hen coop as far as the provincial government was concerned. The voters demanded immediate action, and there was an election in the offing.[12] But it was not the CPR that got things going. It was the dominion government, which was set afire by two sparks in the Canadian railway world brighter than any that flew from the steel wheels.

On January 27, 1898, Major James Morrow Walsh of the North-West Mounted Police, the first commissioner of the Yukon Territory, received a letter from the Honourable Clifford Sifton, minister of the Interior for the government of Canada, which contained the following paragraph:

> We signed a contract yesterday for the construction of a railway from the Stikine River to Teslin Lake. The contract is in the hands of Messrs. Mackenzie and Mann, and they are to build a wagon road in six weeks, with stopping places every 25 miles, and have a railway in operation by September 1st. You will be able to take a steamboat on the river next September and come out like a Christian.[13]

Not mentioned was the inclusion of a river and lake service in the undertaking. This inclusion enabled the dominion government to designate it as a project linking a province and a territory, which made it legal for Ottawa to fund it after the necessary legislation was passed. There was a steamboat built and put on the lake—the *Anglian* was launched at the south end of Teslin Lake on June 13, 1898—and twenty miles of wagon road were built from Glenora heading for Teslin Lake that summer. The road and the steamer were built by the Teslin Transportation Company, W. Mackenzie and D. Mann, proprietors.[14]

Whether Sifton included in his notification to Walsh the condition that all of this was subject to the passage of the necessary legislation is not known, but the last step of the legislative process, approval from the Canadian Senate, was not achieved, and one more proposal for railway construction in the northwest collapsed. Sifton must have been very sure of the passage of his legislation to have written in such manner to Walsh, and the final refusal by the senators must have been an acute embarrassment to the Laurier Liberals.

If they put away the poker table following Sifton's rather premature announcement, they had to bring it out again very quickly because after all of this there was still one more player willing to step up and try his luck. That gambler was none other than Michael Haney, the same man who had bulldozed the CPR mainline construction through for Andrew Onderdonk. Early in 1898 Haney had convinced a British financial empire to sponsor a rail line from Skagway over White Pass to the head of Yukon River navigation at Whitehorse rapids, to be known as the White Pass and Yukon Railway. By the month of May it was under way. The 110-mile narrow-gauge line was a reality by the end of July 1900, and it was, and still is, one of the great successes of northern transportation.[15] It was a nip-and-tuck decision at the time, and it certainly weighed against the government's taking any action towards reversing the Senate rejection of the Mackenzie and Mann proposal.

On the Stikine, everyone was stunned by the reversal, and there was immediate criticism of the government's failure to act. It was a crushing blow to the CPR. But even though the railway scouted out the route initially, it is worth noting that the venture capital that was put on the table belonged to the taxpayer, not the railway company. The CPR was not going to build this railway, which indicated that the boardroom in Montreal might have had some doubts from the start about the route's viability. The company was anxious to cash in on quick profits from the river service but not to take the risks of investing in the rail line.[16]

Viewed in the light of present times, following the demise of the sternwheeler, it is clear the proposal was never viable. The 120-mile stretch of the Stikine River below Telegraph Creek to tidewater had all the negative aspects of any glacier-fed stream, subject to the unpredictability of glaciers; in addition to this it was frozen in its upper reaches for many months, and where the valley reached the ocean in Alaska there was not even a community reachable by rail. Fort Wrangell was on Wrangell Island, separated from the mainland by a wide body of salt water. The White Pass route was the right solution, and if nothing else the whole exercise

Michael J. Haney could well be described as the unsung hero of railway construction in the Pacific Northwest. As well as ramming through the construction of the CPR line from Yale to Craigellachie in the 1880s and contributing such improvements in technique as prefabrication of bridge spans, he also went on to build the CPR's southern B.C. line, from the Blairmore area near Crowsnest Pass to Kootenay Lake, in the record time of one year at the end of the 1890s. Concurrent with this he engineered the financing for the White Pass and Yukon Railway from Skagway to Whitehorse, starting off as the contractor for labour and ending up as the contractor of record. Following this he became involved in the Klondike Mines Railway, running from Dawson for thirteen miles to Grand Forks; then in 1906 in partnership he started the building of the Copper River and Northwestern Railway in Alaska from the coast to the Kennecott Mine, by his report a much more difficult job than the White Pass & Yukon—if that were possible! Quite enough mountain railway building for one man's lifetime.

Telegraph Creek on the Stikine River was another early community spawned by gold.

at the Stikine proved the value of the Canadian system of senate approval.

When it all collapsed there was nothing to be done at the far end but to move on, and the gold seekers at the top of the trail who got there just a little bit late and missed the last boat to Dawson, which left early in the fall, or those intent upon working on the railway had no option other than to make the 137-mile trek back to Glenora, then hike another 120 miles to the coast. As they walked across the muskeg and brush and down the Stikine on its solid ice surface—and nearly froze to death in the chill winds—they bitterly cursed the senators. Their only comfort and sustenance were the supply dumps that had been put out the summer before in advance of the road and rail construction. This had been done with teams of horses, first pulling wagons and then dragging carts. The horses were later put up for sale at Teslin, where most of them were butchered.[17]

Among the men retreating in despair was one whose fate was ordained by a higher authority than that of the unwilling senate

White Pass runs through the Coast Mountains and is less steep in approach than Chilkoot Pass, but steep enough. It was discovered by Captain William Moore and became notorious for the number of horses killed traversing it in winter in the frenzy of the Klondike gold rush.

The Ogilvie, *named after William Ogilvie, surveyor and author of* Early Days on the Yukon, *flies the CPR's British Columbia Lake and River Service flag, but it never saw the home waters of that company. It made several trips to Telegraph Creek on the Stikine River, established the best speed on the run, and was the best boat ever on the river.*

appointees in Ottawa. Norman Lee was a rancher and a trader who drove 200 head of cattle from his home ranch in the Cariboo overland to Hazelton, then by the Telegraph Trail to Telegraph Creek, and on up the Teslin Trail to Teslin Lake. In the fall of 1898 he slaughtered his beasts and loaded the beef onto scows. He set off in good spirits, heading for Dawson on what he thought was an easy lake-and-river route. It normally was. A few miles down the lake, however, a sudden squall sank the scows, and all his hopes and expectations went down with them. Lee returned on foot to Fort Wrangell, caught a ship to Seattle, and arrived back home penniless.[18]

When work started on the White Pass and Yukon Railway, the CPR immediately disposed of the twelve sternwheelers it had built or purchased for the Stikine venture. The company had planned on a total of twenty, proof positive that it had believed this would be the main avenue to the Klondike (and also that rivercraft were a much more mobile investment than a rail line).

The events leading to the start of work on the White Pass and Yukon must have brought bitter gall to the CPR when it heard of them. Apparently a Canadian civil engineer by the name of Michael Beamish and a representative of an English financial empire called Close Brothers got together to consider financing a railway. They hiked over the first twenty miles of the route through White Pass early in March of 1898, and they were eating in a restaurant in Skagway after agreeing that it was quite impossible when in walked Michael Haney. (Another version places Sir Thomas Tancred, the noted British civil and hydraulic engineer, later involved in Klondike dredging, at the meeting, ignores the Canadian engineer, and moves the meeting place to a bar.) It is quite probable that he had cleverly arranged the meeting. Haney, just back from building the CPR line from Crowsnest Pass to Kootenay Lake in southern B.C., had also looked over the route and was sure that it could be done. He successfully convinced them to go ahead and started off in May 1898 as the contractor for labour, ending up as the contractor of record. He had four difficult miles done in two months, and the 110 miles completed by July 29, 1900. Nothing could have convinced the CPR more completely than this that it was on a lost cause on the Stikine.[19]

The significance of this meeting and the decision made at it is not widely recognized. Had they not occurred it is very possible that the narrow-gauge rail line from Glenora to Teslin Lake would have gone ahead, and that would have made a great deal of difference to the future of the northern third of British Columbia. For one thing, instead of a distribution centre at Whitehorse and a Native village at Teslin, their roles might have been reversed. The lands surrounding Teslin Village have always been superior for settlement to those of Whitehorse Rapids.

To further complicate the situation, if such was possible, two prospectors from Juneau, Alaska, found gold near Atlin Lake in August 1898. When word reached Skagway it is said that 80 percent of the workers on the railway downed tools.[20] They were soon replaced, but the rail workers continued to rotate, with those who had earned a grubstake moving on to the goldfields. The gold rush at Atlin Lake brought a lake steamer into service there, the *Scotia,* and it operated until 1918 before it was hauled out. Its remains lay mouldering on the beach in front of town before going up in smoke in 1967.[21]

In a rather shamefaced way, Ottawa announced that it would finance the building of a four-foot-wide trail from Telegraph Creek to Atlin, with an offshoot to Teslin, and this was done.[22] Alongside it the government installed a telegraph line connecting with Quesnel via a resurrected line on the Collins alignment. On September 20, 1901, the Yukon Telegraph Line became operative. It was 1900 miles long and connected Dawson City to Ashcroft, where it met the CPR telegraph. There was already a line to Skagway.

Another interesting communication development in the north, but further to the east, took place between 1897 and 1907. The North-West Mounted Police roughed out a trail and further on a bush road—in other words a widened trail lacking permanent bridges—from Athabasca Landing in Alberta through to the Finlay River, and by its valley up the Rocky Mountain Trench towards Lower Post, where Dease River enters the Liard. They got quite far ahead with this, and they also built 97 miles of wagon road before the whole thing was dropped following a change of mind in Ottawa. While this trail would have permitted easier patrolling in winter, maintenance would have been much more difficult than construction for such an undertaking, and the police were not set up for that. This trail never was maintained, and most of what remained of it disappeared under the reservoir of the Peace River Dam in the 1960s.

The dominion government did not excel in finishing things in that period, and it was also rather cheap, paying Mackenzie and Mann the inadequate sum of $328,508.30 for all their efforts, and this through the Exchequer Court. The two of them did much better out of Premier Turner.

Despite the CPR's immediate retreat from the river after the Stikine route collapsed, the withdrawal from the Stikine was not complete. Four paddlewheelers stayed on, and summer service to

This century-old photo shows Atlin, one of the northwestern B.C. communities that came into existence with a gold rush. It was served by the Atlin Road leading to Whitehorse, one of the earliest roads in the north.

The Scotia is shown before the spectacular scenery of Atlin Lake's west side, some of the least-viewed mountain magnificence in British Columbia. The little steamer came with the Atlin gold rush, outlasted it, and ran until 1918, when it was beached in front of town and mouldered there for half a century.

THE SAME WEEK, THE NEXT YEAR

Glaciers are usually very picturesque when viewed at a distance on a mountaintop, but for the men looking after the roads of British Columbia they are not nearly as beautiful, especially when they are close by.

In 1959 the Department of Highways commenced surveying for a road through Bear Pass to connect Stewart to the planned road from Kitwanga to Watson Lake (see the map "The Alaska Highway and Its Offshoots" in Chapter 3). The surveyors contemplated Bear Glacier, which lay across their way through Bear Pass. They realized that the glacier was in retreat and that only the tongue lay across the pass. It was much reduced from what it had been when Donald Mann and William Mackenzie looked at it in 1897 and promptly gave up their plans to build a railway through the pass and on to Teslin Lake. The men challenging it 62 years later had no intention of giving up. They also knew that if they waited for only a few years more they might find that their problem had removed itself.

But that was for the future. Meanwhile they had to get past the ice with an access road. So they built a rough road up the mountainside around the tip of the glacier's tongue, a road that had to climb a considerable distance above the pass at its highest point.

Like most glaciers blocking valleys, Bear Glacier held back a small lake on the higher side. These lakes are called kettle lakes (and we shall soon see why). Such lakes often float small icebergs formed when a piece of the glacier splits off, or calves as they say, and this lake had its small iceberg of the usual attractive aquamarine colouring. From it the lake drew its name, Berg Lake.

In 1960 the Department started building an improved road up the valley and a new road through Bear Canyon, which lay just below the pass and previously only contained a trail. By the fall of 1961 this road was completed to its first phase, which made it sufficient for construction access.

Glacier tongues are not solid ice, especially on glaciers that are receding. Although the shell is solid, underneath it is like a sponge soaked in water, the water penetrating from the kettle lake. The pressure of the water on the glacier is in direct ratio to the depth of the lake. In the fall of 1961, in the third week of October after a long summer and a warm fall, that tongue was greatly weakened by melting from within. When a period of heavy rain raised Berg Lake to its maximum height, the tongue broke under the pressure of water, a fifty-foot-wide hole formed, and the lake gushed out.

This is why they are called kettle lakes—every now and again nature pours them out. In some cases the lake floats the glacier and the water escapes under it; in this case it broke open a hole. Berg Lake could have been classed as a water closet lake rather than a kettle lake, because it drained itself completely within a few hours that night, as if someone had pulled the plug.

Fortunately there was no one on that road late at night as the water flushed out Bear Canyon right down to the bedrock, and the roadway that had been built that summer simply disappeared. Below the canyon the valley widened out and the rush of water, now filled with debris, spread its contents in a glacial fan—this is the way that glacial till is formed.

Winter immediately set in and the tongue was covered with snow, which filled in the hole. The freezing temperatures put a layer of ice over it. In the spring the glacier looked very much as it did before. Precipitation filled the lake up and there was even another small iceberg. The Department replaced the road, but only built a rough tote road this time. The crew also dug a ditch in the ice across the glacier that summer, using a bulldozer with grousers fixed to its tracks so it would not slip, in order to lower the lake level in hopes that it would not repeat its disappearing act.

But this was all to no avail. Come the third week of October 1962, the hole opened up and out went the lake and the road—the same week, the next year.

The following summer and fall, with further work on the ditch and with the accelerating departure of the tongue, the lake never formed at all. In a few years the glacier was right out of the pass, and the final roadway was built and paved. Road users comfortably driving through the pass sometimes notice a rough and rocky road alongside theirs. It is built crazily up the mountainside and down again, and they wonder at the sight. They also admire the beautiful glacier towering above them on the other side of the pass. Roadworkers do not share this admiration. They wonder what it will do next.

Telegraph Creek from Fort Wrangell continued until 1916. After that, two trips by sternwheeler a summer, with trips by large dugout canoes occasionally in times between, sufficed for many years. Then interest in the area increased, and by 1952 an old Yukon skipper had a weekly service in operation using twin-screw diesel tunnel boats carrying 30 tons of freight and fitted out with comfortable staterooms sufficient for up to twelve passengers. (Tunnel boats have recesses in the hull into which the propellers can be withdrawn in shallow water.)[23]

In accordance with the theory that it is an ill wind that blows no one some good, the Stikine fiasco was a godsend to the people of the Slocan and Kootenay areas in 1898. As a direct result of it they received the *Minto* and the *Moyie*, the two longest-lasting, and some say the best, sternwheelers of the southern Interior. The more than 1000 separate steel pieces that made up the *Minto*'s riveted steel hull were diverted in transit to Nakusp, and the *Moyie*'s to Nelson, just in time for a launching to coincide with the completion of the CPR line from Lethbridge to Kootenay Landing at the end of the year.[24]

Steel is of course stronger than wood, even Douglas fir, and lasts longer, as these two fine vessels proved, but the wooden hulls of their sister ships deserve respect. The hull planking of the *Keno*, which sits proudly on the bank of the Yukon River beside the main thoroughfare of Dawson City, was measured by the author to be a full three inches in thickness. During the 1890s it is recorded that William West ordered planking for the *Royal City* from the Brunette Sawmill at New Westminster. The planks were of the best Douglas fir and measured 120 feet in length. They were duly delivered to Fort Langley where the boat was built. They were probably three inches thick and eight inches wide. You would have some difficulty obtaining these at your local lumber yard today![25]

During World War II, in 1940, an airport was constructed at Watson Lake, one of the chain of airstrips built to make an air bridge from the rest of the United States to Alaska. The materials for this were brought in by barge to Telegraph Creek and by road and barge from there on. The Telegraph-Dease Lake Road was improved, and three tunnel boats were built at Dease Lake, along with a diesel-powered sternwheeler. The Alaska Highway construction used and then replaced this service in due course.[26] That highway also greatly helped the area, opening it up to tourism and development. As mentioned in Chapter 3, the construction of an asbestos mine at Cassiar in turn brought the Cassiar-Stewart Highway (Highway 37). Asbestos is now a forbidden substance so the mine is closed, but the highway is still there and giving good service.

Another result of all of this, apart from the developments already mentioned, was that a large network of trails in this corner of British Columbia came to be maintained by the B.C. road authority, usually with the help of the Mines Department. Stories are told of honeymooning couples, much hardier in the early 1900s than most are now, hiking from Hazelton to Telegraph Creek, or from there on to Atlin, and making good use of the trailside cabins. How they dealt with the bears is not known. Occasionally they would meet a prospector.

The telegraph trail and its extension to Atlin, and a similar telegraph line and trail built by the dominion government to Port Simpson from Hazelton, both complete with cabins, were of tremendous value to the B.C. Provincial Police, a force highly regarded during its existence from the very start of the province until it was disbanded in 1950. Its forays by dog team in the depth of winter were as much for search and rescue as for law enforcement. The police built a lock-up at Glenora in 1898, a stop-over until the boat came, and it remained as the last building there for many years.[27] The cabins on the trail north from Hazelton were numbered one through nine, while on the Atlin trail they were named after the rivers—Sheslay, Nahlin, Nakina, and Pike (a coincidental honour to Pikey).

The most telling result to the Department of Public Works (and later Highways), besides the huge mileage of trails, was the

This shows the tractors and trailers of a mining outfit travelling on the Telegraph Creek to Dease Lake Road, which was not more than nine or ten feet wide by the look of it. The photograph is undated but was probably taken in the early or mid-1930s, after the DPW's 1920s improvements but before the road was rebuilt in the early 1940s. In the background is the far side of the Stikine River canyon, with the river surface many hundreds of feet below. That face is typical of the canyon, steep, gravelly clay with lava layers in places. The material erodes interminably, with the river constantly washing out the detritus at the toe. It is a very difficult place in which to build anything.

Telegraph Creek to Dease Lake Road, the sole overland link to civilization for the village of Telegraph Creek, which continued to exist as a government centre and RCMP post long after the Alaska Highway made it redundant. This was because the Native people from Iskut Village and other locations were moved to a reserve near Telegraph Creek and did not move back to their traditional centres until Highway 37 was built in the 1960s, after which Dease Lake gained the importance it should have had all along.

The trails crisscrossing this country to the remote lakes and rivers and Native villages remained in existence for many years, but most are now either logging or mining roads or, like old soldiers, have simply faded away. There are many dreams laid to rest with them.

Once World War II came to an end it became obvious that some excellent planning and preparation for highway work had taken place during the war. Under the aegis of two of the most proficient Public Works ministers that B.C. has ever had—Herbert Anscomb and Ernest Carson—the Public Works Ministry came out of the conflict remarkably ready to go to work to build the type of highways that both the postwar vehicles and the public using them required.[28]

After recovering from the spring floods of 1948, the ministry went fully into its postwar rebuilding program as men and materials, along with new and greatly improved earth-moving and rock-handling equipment, came on the scene. By the fall of 1949 the most sought-after highway connection was opened, that from Hope to Princeton. The Hart Highway, linking the rest of B.C. to the Peace River Block, followed a few years later. A start was made on greatly needed improvement of the Trans-Canada route. The golden age of highway building in British Columbia was fully underway, running from the 1950s through the 60s and 70s and terminating midway through the 1980s with the completion of the Coquihalla Highway.[29]

The railways picked up their best handle on survival with the advent of the unit train in the 1970s—which moved huge quantities of freight to a single destination point. The CPR twigged to this first, hauling southeastern coal to Roberts Bank. The BC Railway and the CNR soon followed suit, taking northeastern coal from Tumbler Ridge to Ridley Island.

But the sternwheelers were gone for good.

Two men symbolize the golden years of the sternwheelers in British Columbia: John Irving and William Moore. Irving succeeded his father in paddle-wheeling and dealing. William Moore's career spanned it all—from the arrival of his sternwheeler at Yale in 1858 to the massive Klondike-bound seaborne excursion of 1898. He was the free spirit; he explored the Stikine country, and he did not stop there. After all, there were at least two more avenues into the hinterland from the Pacific even if the Alaska panhandle intervened; these were Taku Inlet and Lynn Canal.

Herbert Anscomb, minister of Public Works from 1942 to 1945, and Ernest Carson, minister from 1945 to 1952, served British Columbia exceedingly well at the end of the war and immediately after it.

There was no indication at all during the last two decades of Moore's half century of following gold strikes in British Columbia that he was any less of an unbelievable character than he was in the first three. It was uncanny how he seemed to anticipate the Klondike strike. His involvement with gold and the Yukon started in 1886, and from that year through to 1891 he prospected the area. He even had a claim on Bonanza Creek, which he lost when he went sternwheeling as he had another man register it. It is said that he discovered White Pass while packing in supplies for the renowned surveyor and explorer William Ogilvie, for whom the Ogilvie Mountains are named. Moore built the first long trestle dock across the mudflats at Skagway in 1888 and he pre-empted 60 acres beside it. He even applied for a charter from the Alaskan authorities for a toll road through his pass, which was refused.

After trading up and down Lynn Canal with his *Flying Dutchman*, in 1896 Moore obtained a contract to deliver mail, summer and winter, by boat or dog team, from Juneau to Fortymile, a settlement 30 miles downstream from Dawson on the Yukon River. While packing on one trail in 50 degrees below zero weather, he was overtaken by some younger men; he later met up with them when they ran out of steam, and he saved them from freezing to death. This was also in 1896 when he was 73 years old. He died in 1909.[30]

Moore's investment in Skagway set him up well for the rest of his days. John Irving on the other hand, although entering into the Yukon scene in great style, sold his Canadian Pacific Navigation Company interests to the CPR, then founded another steamboat company for the Yukon River, which he finally sold to the White Pass & Yukon Railway complete with rivercraft. Thereafter his business success seemed to die with the sternwheelers that he knew so well. One of the conditions of sale of the CPN was that he be given lifetime free transportation on all CPR vessels, and Irving ended up spending most of his time on the ships of his erstwhile competitor, an undignified ending for a great man. He died in 1935 at the age of 84.[31]

But Moore and Irving were not alone. They moved in a company of men and women with vision. Gustavus Blin Wright and Governor James Douglas, Robert Cunningham, Robert Tomlinson, and William Duncan. And the railway men: Charles Hays, Michael Haney, and of course the CPR hierarchy. And how much vision and support came from their wives? The unpretentious Mrs. William Moore, bringing up three sons for him (another died young), while he rushed around in every direction. Amelia Douglas, who kept her head and saved her husband's at the Hudson's Bay Company's Fort St. James in 1828, when Douglas was seized by a group of angry Natives who demanded payment in goods for his life. Then there was Louise Hays, the wife of Charles Melville Hays, the railway genius. She survived the sinking of the *Titanic* when she was conducted to a lifeboat by her husband, accompanied by her married daughter. Hays stayed behind with his son-in-law and his manservant, and they were all lost. Mrs. Hays subsequently refused to sue the White Star Line over the death of her husband, on the basis that Lord Ismay, the White Star chairman, who himself was saved on the last lifeboat, had offered them free passage on the doomed liner, which they had accepted. She met utter disaster with grace and honour, as did her husband.

Men and women like these were worth more to early British Columbia than all the gold they strove so hard to find.

HILL THE MOVER

One of this author's many remarkable memories of working on roads in northern B.C. comes from a trip to inspect three road-construction contracts covering 91 miles of the Cassiar-Stewart Highway south of Dease Lake, which were all under way in 1961. These contracts extended south from the northern end of the highway.

I was speaking to a survey crew on the job, discussing the peacefulness of the remote countryside, the beauty of Eddontenajon Lake—so similar in appearance to Okanagan Lake, the only difference being a lack of about 10 degrees Celsius in the mean annual temperature—and the distance from civilization that meant they could work without the presence of outside traffic.

Suddenly a rather strange object hove into view on the rough tote road giving access to the various contracts, a road only meant for four-wheel-drive vehicles or off-highway dirt movers. The transitman trained his telescope on it and reported that it was a small, yellow, three-axle, semi-trailer truck that looked like a furniture van and that had some lettering on its side. A few minutes later he could read the letters, and he advised us that they spelled out "Hill the Mover."

When he got to us, the driver said he was bound for Telegraph Creek. We informed him that he had missed the turnoff by about 70 miles and he was stunned, as he knew these were not easy miles. With some help he turned his vehicle around and off he went. Why the operator of the ferry across the Stikine River, put there to serve the contractors, did not question him is not clear, except that northern ferrymen are notoriously uncommunicative.

That day and the next were spent looking at the work, and the next evening we reached Good Hope Lake Camp quite late. The camp, which is in fact a depot, is quite close to Cassiar. The next morning we asked the foreman about Hill the Mover, and he told us that they had seen him southbound but not coming out again. This led to a radio enquiry to the Telegraph Creek Highway detachment, and it turned out they had not seen Hill the Mover at all. When we asked whether anyone had been over the Telegraph Creek to Dease Lake road in the last several days, they said no and immediately left to patrol the road. Several hours later they reported back and told the story.

The mover had gone in as far as the Stikine Canyon, to a section of road similar to that shown in the photograph on page 162. Going around an outside curve at full lock, he suddenly realized that his outside driving wheels were heading out into thin air. He stopped. Then he found that he could not back up safely either. He was stuck. He waited for a passing motorist to help him, but no one came. When darkness arrived he put out markers and flares and went to sleep. In the morning there was still no one around, so he took out his axe, cut some poplar trees, and started building a small cribbing in the fashion of others used to support the road. This would provide enough roadway for him to continue. By nightfall he was almost finished, and he believed that the next morning he could fill it up with gravel and get moving again. The next morning help arrived.

The highway crew with their dump truck had the necessary resources to move him over sufficiently, and they unhitched the trailer and directed him to move his tractor unit to a place farther down the hill where he could turn around. They unloaded the contents of the trailer, which were the household effects of an RCMP constable being transferred from Stewart to Telegraph Creek, manhandled the trailer around with the help of the dump truck, hooked it back onto the tractor, and sent him on his way. It was then two full days and two nights since he had first tried to negotiate that treacherous road. Shortly after that the van passed Good Hope Lake Camp at high speed on its way out.

Two trips of the dump truck delivered the constable's belongings to the RCMP station at the Creek.

It seemed that someone at RCMP headquarters in Ottawa had refused to send the household effects out by air or by boat through American waters and had insisted that tenders be called for the 1500-mile overland journey by moving van from Stewart to Telegraph Creek via Prince George, Fort St. John, Watson Lake, and down to Dease Lake via the Yellowhead, Hart, and Alaska highways, but they had not anticipated the curves on that road.

The single-engine de Havilland Otter freight-carrying aircraft, which was the workhorse of the Stewart area for the mining companies in these years, would have covered the 200 air miles between Stewart and Dease Lake in just over two hours, provided Bear Pass was not clouded in as it often was. A local trucker could then have taken the load down from Dease Lake to Telegraph Creek in a similar length of time. By water it was about 300 miles from Stewart to Wrangell, Alaska. There were a number of freight vessels available for this trip, which would have taken about two days. From Wrangell the MV Judith Ann—64 feet, drawing 2.5 feet—regularly pushed a scow carrying groceries up the Stikine River to Telegraph Creek in the 1960s, a trip of 125 miles. This usually took about four days, depending on the state of the river. The 1500-mile trip across B.C. would have taken at least six days; the roads at either end were not easy ones.

If there is another move, and another tender call, one thing is sure: Hill the Mover will not bid again.

Chapter Notes

Introduction

1. More specifically the Fraser and the Nechako Plateaus.

2. When Rupert's Land was extended to the Pacific slope as a result of the Hudson's Bay Company's acquisition of the North West Company in 1821, the HBC gained exclusive rights to New Caledonia and all the North West Company's holdings west of the Rockies. (Rupert's Land was the original Hudson's Bay Company land grant, being all of Canada draining into Hudson's Bay.) The HBC lost its overall land tenure in British Columbia when that land was returned to the Crown upon the creation of the colony in 1858.

Chapter One

1. Stumer, *This Was Klondike Fever.*
2. Stumer, *Klondike Fever*, p. 85; Akrigg, *B.C. Chronicle: 1847-1871*, pp. 254, 383-384; *Encyclopaedia Britannica*, 1960 edition, s.v. "Field, Cyrus West." It is reported that when the overland telegraph company got the go-ahead, an armada of ships set sail from San Francisco, dropping off huge bales of wire and a multitude of insulators at each point of inland access from the ocean right up the Pacific coast to Alaska. At many of these points they also landed survey parties. In British Columbia the boats went up the Fraser, the Skeena, the Nass, the Stikine, and the Taku. Reportedly they even went as far as the mouth of the Yukon and landed at St. Michaels, although how far they went up the river is not known. That party was a year late in hearing that it was all over.
3. Neering, *Continental Dash*, pp.
4. Mackay, "The Collins Overland Telegraph," *BCHQ* 10, no. 3 (1949): p. 207. Surveyor and explorer Michael Byrne of the Collins Overland Telegraph Company is mentioned by Robert C. Coutts

in his *Yukon Places and Names* as "being probably the first white man to see Atlin Lake." He reached the south end of it in his wide sweep north from Hazelton in 1866.

5. Orchard, *Martin: The Story of a Young Fur Trader*, pp. 68-69.

6. Downs, *Paddlewheels on the Frontier*, vol. 1, pp. 61-62; Mackay, "Collins Overland Telegraph," p. 207.

7. Akrigg, *B.C. Chronicle: 1847-1871*, pp. 383-384; Ramsey, *Ghost Towns of British Columbia*, p. 214.

8. Ormsby, *British Columbia: A History*, pp. 220-221; Large, *The Skeena: River of Destiny*, pp. 49-50.

9. Downs, *Paddlewheels*, vol. 1, p. 49.

10. West, "The *B.X.* and the Rush to Fort George," *BCHQ* 13, nos. 3 and 4 (1949), pp. 138-9; Hutchinson, *The Fraser*, p. 156; Morice, *History of the Northern Interior of B.C.*; Downs, *Paddlewheels*, vol. 2, pp. 65-66; Hacking, "B.C. Steamboat Days 1870-1883," *BCHQ* 11, no. 2 (1947), pp. 73-74.

11. Chittenden, *Travels in British Columbia*, p. 47; Downs, *Paddlewheels*, vol. 1, pp. 49-50; Downs, *Wagon Road North*, p. 27; West, *Stagecoach and Sternwheel Days in the Cariboo and Central B.C.*, pp. 38-39.

12. Runnalls, "Boom Days in Prince George," *BCHQ* 8, no. 4 (1944), pp. 284-306; Ormsby, *British Columbia*, p. 359

13. The photographs are BCARS nos. 10544 and 27411.

14. Downs, *Paddlewheels*, vol. 1, p. 53

15. Lord, *Alex Lord's British Columbia*, pp. 71-74; West, *Stagecoach and Sternwheel*, pp. 34-94.

16. Downs, *Paddlewheels*, vol. 1, pp. 52-59; Kopas, *Packhorses to the Pacific*, pp. 69-70.

17. Downs, *Paddlewheels*, vol. 1, pp. 54-56.

18. Ibid., pp. 52-59.

19. Kopas, *Packhorses*, pp. 9, 42-43.

20. Ibid., pp. 73, 79-94.

21. Ibid., p. 95.

22. Downs, *Paddlewheels*, vol. 1, pp. 52-59.

23. Harvey, *The Coast Connection*, p. 75.

24. Orchard, *Martin*, pp. 68-69; Chittenden, *Travels*, p. 47.

25. The source for the boxed item entitled "The Prizewinner" is "The *B.X.* and the Rush to Fort George" by Willis J. West, a 97-page article in the *B.C. Historical Quarterly* 13, nos. 3 and 4, pp. 129-226.

This is also the source for the Winston Six photo caption. This article is a most valuable historical document. Mr. West was the superintendent for the B.C. Express Company in the Cariboo during the sternwheeler times, and he describes trips through Cottonwood Canyon and Fort George Canyon with Captain O.F. Browne, and through the Grand Canyon of the Fraser with Captain J.E. Bucey.

West details the lamentable closure of the river to sternwheelers by the GTP contractor in 1913 in defiance of a Board of Railway Commissioners Order, with the connivance of the dominion government. He relates the strange coincidences of the trip through the courts. He also outlines the land boom in Fort George, and tells of the Hammond brothers, who built a sternwheeler (named for George's son and heir) for the sole purpose of proving that the Nechako River was a sternwheeler centre as mentioned in their advertising, which it was not.

West goes on to tell of the political patronage surrounding the award of postal contracts in the Cariboo involving Steve Tingley and an entrant from Ontario, Charles V. Millar. The latter took over from the former after a change of government in Ottawa in 1896, Conservative to Liberal. West tells of Tingley accepting reality and co-operating with Millar and selling him the B.C. Express Company at a reasonable price. Millar turned out to be a good thing for the Cariboo: for one thing, it is apparent that he hired W.J. West.

Chapter Two

1. B.C. Archives and Records Services, *Kwakiutl,* Our Native People series, vol. 7, pp. 8-18, 25-31; Woodcock, *British Columbia: A History of the Province,* pp. 3-4, 15-22, 50-60.
2. Hardy, *From Sea Unto Sea,* pp. 461-463.
3. Robinson, *Building An Historic Railway: The Memoirs of Henry J. Cambie,* p. 103; Large, *Skeena,* pp. 135-136.
4. Woodcock, *British Columbia,* pp. 183-184.
5. Ormsby, *British Columbia,* pp. 345-347.
6. Large, *Skeena,* pp. 28, 44-47.
7. Gold was found in the Omineca River area in 1869, reached initially from Fort St. James. In 1870 Edgar Dewdney surveyed

improvements and extension of the old Hudson's Bay Company trail from Hazelton to Babine Lake, and the miners travelled it and Indian trails to Takla Lake and on to Manson Creek. Dewdney also located a trail from Stuart Lake northwards to Manson Creek in 1871, the year that the gold finds peaked. There was a ferry service for the goldseekers across Takla Lake, and a bridge was built across the Babine River. The miners either hired Indian canoes or bought them to reach Hazelton from Port Simpson. This 170-mile hike from Hazelton to Manson Creek was probably the first continuous transportation route across central B.C. The country east of the Hogem Range was noted as fine land on Joseph Trutch's map of 1871, but those who have been there in the spring find it notable mostly for the black flies. These were stalwart travellers. They thought Omineca was another Barkerville, but it was not. Gold production was spotty and strong for a few years, and then it was over.

8. Large, *Skeena*, pp. 28-43 passim; Downs, *Paddlewheels*, vol. 1, p. 63.
9. Downs, *Paddlewheels*, vol. 2, pp. 65-66.
10. Large, *Skeena*, pp. 114-115.
11. Downs, *Paddlewheels*, vol. 2, p. 8.
12. Large, *Skeena*, pp. 28-43; Downs, *Paddlewheels*, vol. 1, p. 63.
13. Large, *Skeena*, pp. 81-86.
14. Akrigg, *H.M.S. Virago in the Pacific*, p. 123. There is a report that a British man-of-war was overcome by the Haidas near Masset at some time in history. A road crew's discovery of an ancient gun barrel, marked with what appeared to be a royal crest and buried in the sand beside a road on the Masset Indian reserve in the late 1950s, gives this report credence. An attempt to have this sent to the Provincial Museum was thwarted by the Haida tribal council, which wished to retain its ill-gotten prize. It is said the vessel might have been the HMS *Bluebottle*.
15. Large, *Skeena*, pp. 81-86; Orchard, *Martin*, p. 41.
16. Large, *Skeena*, pp. 114-115; Orchard, *Martin*, p. 38.
17. Large, *Skeena*, p. 147.
18. Walker, *Bacon, Beans 'n Brave Hearts*, p. 48
19. Hardy, *Sea Unto Sea*, p. 461.
20. Lord, *Lord's B.C.*, pp. 61-68.
21. Large, *Skeena*, pp. 166-168.
22. DPW Annual Report, 1942-43, p. O10; Annual Report, 1943-44, pp. Q6, Q28; Annual Report, 1944-45, p. O27.

23. DPW Annual Report, 1929-30, pp. T22, T150. Farley's *Atlas of British Columbia* shows the Nass as the seventh largest river in B.C. and the Skeena as the fifth following the Fraser, Columbia, Peace and Liard, with the Stikine in between. The drainage area of the Skeena is 42,000 sq. km.; the Nass, 21,000; and the Fraser, 230,000.

Chapter Three

1. Farley, *Atlas of B.C.*, p. 13.
2. Bowes, ed., *The Peace River Chronicles*, pp. 13, 221, 228, 240, 260.
3. Berton, *The National Dream*, pp. 47-51, 150, 212.
4. Pike, "A Winter Ordeal" in *Peace River Chronicles*, ed. Bowes, pp. 154-174.
5. Fryer, "Sternwheeler days on the Peace River," in *Pioneer Days in British Columbia*, vol. 2, ed. Downs, pp. 121-127.
6. Kelsey, "Red Powell and His First Airline," pp. 470-472; Baskine, "Dawson Creek and the Alaska Highway," p.473, in *Peace River Chronicles*, ed. Bowes.
7. Ibid.; Brebner, *The Alaska Highway*, pp. 51-62.
8. Swannell, "A Diary of the Bedaux Expedition," pp. 449-457; Lamarque, "Making Trail for M. Bedaux," pp. 439-448; Smythe, "An Expedition to the Lloyd George Mountains," pp. 483-484, all contained in *Peace River Chronicles*, ed. Bowes; Fryer, "The Bedaux Expedition," in *Pioneer Days in British Columbia*, vol. 4, ed. Downs, pp. 74-79.
9. Brebner, *Alaska Highway*, pp. 7-12.
10. Ibid.
11. Material for the map and item "A Long Way Around" was taken from the article by Harold W. Richardson entitled "Alcan: America's Glory Road I," which appeared in the *Engineering News-Record* of December 17, 1942, p. 39.
12. Brebner, *Alaska Highway*, pp. 11-12.
13. Ibid., pp. 19-21; Baskine, "Dawson Creek," in *Peace River Chronicles*, ed. Bowes, pp. 475-481.
14. Young, *The Fort Nelson Story*, pp. 58-63. In February 1941, long before Pearl Harbour, an Edmonton contractor led what was called a caterpillar train out of Fort St. John, building a winter road to Old Fort Nelson to initiate the construction of the Fort Nelson Airport, part of the North West Staging air transport agreement

between Canada and the United States. When the Alcan highway
started up, that airport was still under construction. It was soon
complete.

15. Brebner, *Alaska Highway*, pp. 29-31.

16. Richardson, "Alcan: America's Glory Road II," *Engineering News-
Record*, January 14, 1943, p 138 (BCARS). There were a total of
54 contractors, 13 of them Canadian and 4 of them management
contractors, one of these Canadian, by name R. Melville Smith,
Toronto. The others from Canada were Emil Anderson
Construction Co.; Bond Construction Co.: Campbell
Construction Co.; Curran and Briggs Ltd.; Don Construction Co.;
Dufferin Paving Co. Ltd.; W.H. Harvey and Sons; A.E. Jupp
Construction Co. Ltd.; Wallace A. Mackay Ltd.; Storms
Construction Co. Ltd.; Tomlinson Construction Co.; Carswell
Sand and Gravel. Of these contractors, several went on to bid and
work on the Hope-Princeton and Hart highways once their
construction was put to tender at war's end. These included Emil
Anderson, Campbell, Storms, and Tomlinson. Their introduction
to B.C. by way of the Alaska Highway work was a great advantage
to the province. One name was conspicuous by its absence—
General Construction Co. Ltd. That company was engaged at that
time in the improvement of the Telegraph to Dease Lake Road and
other northern roads.

17. Brebner, *Alaska Highway*, pp. 31-32, 67, 70.

18. Ibid., pp. 43-53; Ministry of Highways (MoH) Annual Report,
1957-58, p. G11.

19. Brebner, *Alaska Highway*, pp. 11-12.

20. MoH Annual Report, 1976-77, p. 5. The national government
contributed to the cost of the Cassiar-Stewart Highway under the
Agreement for Western Northlands Highways, signed with B.C.
in March 1977. The federal government put up $15 million, mainly
for this highway, to be matched by the province. The agreement
lapsed on March 31, 1979.

21. Young, *Fort Nelson*, p. 183. Gerri Young tells us that soon after the
Canadian Army took over the maintenance of the Alaska Highway
in 1946, a group of mechanics of the Royal Canadian Electrical
and Mechanical Engineers, employed at Mile 297 maintaining
vehicles, began prospecting in the area near Lower Post on their
days off. Vic Sittler, Bob Kirk, and Hi Nelson discovered a strange

mineral and discussed it with another prospector who wanted nothing to do with it. They filed claims on it anyway. It was asbestos, and there was a mountain of it. Thus the Cassiar Asbestos Mine came into being. The RCEME men sold their claims to an Ontario company and did not become millionaires, but they did become financially independent.

22. The Shakwak Highway Improvement Agreement was an understanding between the U.S. Department of Transportation, Federal Highway Administration, and the Yukon and B.C. governments, reached in 1977.

23. Of interest was another transportation venture springing from the Alaska Highway in the late 1950s. Riverboats and barges were used to move mostly oil products down the Fort Nelson, the Liard, and the Mackenzie rivers to Inuvik on the Mackenzie delta. This lasted for a number of years, starting from Old Fort Nelson on the Fort Nelson River, which is just a few miles from new Fort Nelson on the highway. See the aside "A Long Way Around."

24. Ormsby, *British Columbia*, p. 399.

25. These figures are taken from the Report of the British Columbia Railway Inquiry of 1977, led by Justice Lloyd MacKenzie. This report is available from the provincial government.

26. Shaw, "A Journalist Reports," in *Peace River Chronicles*, ed. Bowes, pp. 525-529. The W-G BCD Company allied itself to the International Power and Engineering Consultants (IPEC) of Vancouver, which later became an adjunct of B.C. Hydro, who built the dam.

27. Harrington, "A Visit to Hudson Hope," in *Peace River Chronicles*, ed. Bowes, p. 498.

28. Bowes, ed., "Introduction," *Peace River Chronicles*, p. 17.

29. Fryer, "Bedaux Expedition," in *Pioneer Days in British Columbia*, vol. 4, ed. Downs, pp. 76-79.

Chapter Four

1. Cairns, *Notes on Road History of British Columbia*, p. 20.
2. Harvey, *Coast Connection*, p. 44.
3. Hacking, *Captain William Moore*, pp. 10-32.
4. Ibid.; Downs, *Paddlewheels*, vol. 2, pp. 62-63.
5. Turner, *The Pacific Princesses*, p. 4.

6. Ramsey, *Ghost Towns*, p. 77.
7. Ibid., pp. 77-87.
8. Johnston, *Beyond the Rockies*, p. 7; Dunae, *Gentlemen Emigrants*, pp. 115-122.
9. Margaret Ormsby summarizes a UBC student's thesis, "Disposal of Crown Lands in British Columbia, 1871-1913" (*British Columbia*, p. 309). Robert E. Cail researched Lands Branch records and relates how in 1899 two Victoria, B.C., merchants received a railway charter for a line from Yellowhead Pass to Nanaimo, B.C. The land amounted to 14 million acres, obtained even though they never turned a sod. All that was necessary was for them to submit a form showing the address of the registered office, the directors of the company, and the termini of the line. This then required the support of a private member of Parliament for a Railway Bill, and that of a cabinet member and a senator for a Supply Statute, and the deed was done. Premier Robson is credited with the removal of water rights and mineral rights from these railway grants (he got in trouble with the removal of mineral rights in the area around Nelson), but Ormsby reports that mineral rights went with this grant.

   Of interest to this, though probably coincidental, is part of an article by Marjorie C. Holmes on Royal Commissions, found in *BCHQ* 8, no. 4 (1944): p. 321. She describes a Royal Commission formed under the Public Inquiries Act from a resolution brought by Smith Curtis, MLA for Rossland, on March 19, 1902. The resolution was brought against James Dunsmuir and certain members of his cabinet regarding money and lands sought in respect to a planned rail line from Bute Inlet to Yellowhead Pass involving the Esquimalt and Nanaimo Railway and the Comox and Cape Scott Railway (a line that existed on paper only). The Commission was adjourned before doing anything, and there the record ceases.
10. Ormsby, *British Columbia*, p. 333.
11. Turner, *Sternwheelers and Steam Tugs*, pp. 72-73.
12. Ormsby, *British Columbia*, pp. 318-319.
13. Downs, ed., *Pioneer Days*, vol. 3, pp. 144-151. This section is about Guy Lawrence, who worked on the Yukon Telegraph Line and wrote several articles about it; Turner, *Sternwheelers*, pp. 73-74. The Yukon Territory was not officially created until June 1898. Walsh did not return to Dawson until May 1898, by which time he had decided to resign.

14. Turner, *Sternwheelers*, pp. 73-74; Lindo, ed., *Making History*, pp. 70-76. This section is about W.G. Crisp, who managed fur posts for the HBC in the Cassiar District early in this century. He wrote often in the HBC publication *The Beaver*.

15. Phillips, *Canada's Railways*, pp. 72-76.

16. Turner, *Sternwheelers*, pp. 72-74.

17. Downs, ed., *Pioneer Days*, vol. 3 (Guy Lawrence), pp. 140-151; Lindo, ed., *Making History* (W.G. Crisp), p. 72.

18. Lee, *Klondike Cattle Drive*, pp. 33-78; Downs, ed., *Pioneer Days*, vol. 3 (Kathleen Telford), p. 13.

19. Phillips, *Canada's Railways*, pp. 72-76; Stumer, *Klondike Fever*, p. 46.

20. Downs, *Paddlewheels*, vol. 2, p. 74.

21. Ibid., p. 76.

22. Downs, ed., *Pioneer Days*, vol. 3 (Guy Lawrence), p. 144; Kelly, ed., *The Mounties as They Saw Themselves*, pp. 168-175. In the Spring 1986 issue of *The RCMP Quarterly*, as transcribed in *The Mounties*, Divisional Commander W.H. Kelly contributes an article entitled "The Darling Patrol." It tells of a 1910 trip that Sergeant John Darling of the RNWMP made from Athabasca Landing, Alberta, to Fort St. John, B.C., by trail. He re-established the first mileposts of a bush road built by Superintendent Charles Constantine, RNWMP, five years before, and then followed the traces of it from Fort St. John to Fort Grahame on the Finlay River (now inundated by Lake Williston). Darling found it to be totally unused and full of deadfalls, which he cleared away. He reported that the bridges were all originally made of poplar and were fully rotted out. He left the bush road at Fort Grahame and went due west by Indian trails to the Telegraph Trail, which he followed to Atlin and from there to Whitehorse and out. The Constantine bush road was never again referred to or used by the RNWMP and continued in total disuse until flooded over.

23. Lindo, ed., *Making History* (W.G. Crisp), p. 73; Hoagland, *Notes from the Century Before*, p. 34.

24. Turner, *Sternwheelers*, pp. 99-100

25. Waite, *The Langley Story*, p. 157.

26. Lindo, ed., *Making History* (W.G. Crisp), p. 75.

27. Downs, ed., *Pioneer Days*, vol. 4 (Guy Lawrence), pp. 26-31; Downs, ed., *Pioneer Days*, vol. 2 (Francis Dickie), pp. 141-145; Clark, ed., *B.C. Provincial Police Stories*, vol. 3 (Constable J.W. Todd, RCMP),

pp. 126-129 (Todd was in charge of the RCMP Telegraph Creek Detachment from 1942-44.); Hoagland, *Notes*, p. 6.

28. Harvey, *Coast Connection*, pp. 126-132. The judgment by the author that Anscomb (minister from 1942 to 1946) and Carson (1946 to 1952) were two of the best, if not *the* best, ministers of Public Works (or Highways) is not casually arrived at. The author served under Ernie Carson from 1948 to 1952 and fully experienced the respect all had for him. Carson was from a pioneer family in the Lillooet area, prominent in the first years of the province. He travelled constantly around the Interior during his time in office, talking to residents everywhere. His word was his bond and he never gave out false hope—rather extraordinary qualities in a politician.

Knowledge of Herbert Anscomb comes from a reading of his diary as minister of Public Works during the war years. He also travelled widely, at a time when that was not easy. One trip to the Peace River Block at the height of the war required special permission from the U.S. authorities to enter their country so he could drive round to Alberta and receive gasoline en route. Then he had to abandon his car to get to Grande Prairie by rail, and from there travel by car—or trail! The trials of getting to the Peace River from Victoria certainly must have influenced Premier John Hart when he heard of them and probably spurred him on to build the Hart Highway to that forgotten corner of B.C. as soon as the war was over. Anscomb's skill in dealing with public meetings where people were demanding better roads everywhere in the province, when wartime conditions meant that he had neither men, materials, nor money to do anything, was also extraordinary. He did plan ahead, however, as became obvious later. He writes extremely well in his diary, which merits publication.

29. Harvey, *Coast Connection*, pp. 135-207.

30. Downs, *Paddlewheels*, vol. 2, p. 67; Hutchinson, *Fraser*, p. 155.

31. Turner, *The Pacific Princesses*, pp. 3-12.

32. Hacking, *Prince Ships of Northern B.C.*, pp. 36, 38.

BIBLIOGRAPHY

Akrigg, G.V.P. and Helen B. *British Columbia Chronicle: 1847-1871.* Vancouver: Discovery Press, 1977.

————. *1001 British Columbia Place Names.* Vancouver: Discovery Press, 1969.

————. *H.M.S. Virago in the Pacific 1851-1855.* Victoria: Sono Nis Press, 1992.

Berton, Pierre. *Klondike.* Toronto: McClelland & Stewart, 1958.

————. *The National Dream.* Toronto: McClelland & Stewart, 1970.

Bowes, Gordon E., ed. *Peace River Chronicles.* Vancouver: Prescott Publishing Co., 1963.

Brebner, Phyllis Lee. *The Alaska Highway.* Erin, ON: The Boston Mills Press, 1985.

B.C. Archives and Records Services. *Kwakiutl.* British Columbia Heritage Series: Our Native Peoples. Series 1 Vol. 7. Victoria: B.C. Department of Education, 1971.

B.C. Department of Public Works/Department of Highways/Ministry of Highways Annual Reports 1929/30, 1942/43, 43/44, 44/45, 76/77

Cairns, H.L. *Notes on Road History of British Columbia.* Victoria: DPW Archives.

Chittenden, Newton H. *Travels in British Columbia.* Vancouver: Gordon Soules Book Publishers, 1984—original 1882.

Clark, Cecil, ed. *B.C. Provincial Police Stories.* Vol. 3. Surrey, B.C.: Heritage House Publishing Co. Ltd., 1993.

Coutts, Robert C. *Yukon Places and Names.* Sidney, B.C.: Gray's Publishing Ltd., 1980.

Downs, Art. *Paddlewheels on the Frontier.* Volumes One & Two. Surrey, B.C.: Foremost Publishing Ltd., 1971. Republished in one volume as *British Columbia-Yukon Sternwheel Days.* Surrey, B.C.: Heritage House Publishing Co. Ltd., 1992.

————. *Wagon Road North*. Quesnel: Northwest Digest Ltd., 1960/ 61. Fourth revised edition from Surrey, B.C.: Heritage House Publishing Co. Ltd., 1993.

————, ed. *Pioneer Days in British Columbia*. Volumes 1 to 4. Surrey, B.C.: Heritage House Publishing Co. Ltd., 1977.

Dunae, Patrick A. *Gentlemen Emigrants*. Vancouver: Douglas & McIntyre, 1981.

Farley, Albert L. *Atlas of British Columbia*. Vancouver: UBC Press, 1979.

Fetherling, Douglas. *The Gold Crusades 1849-1929*. Toronto: Macmillan of Canada, 1988.

Hacking, Norman. *Captain William Moore*. Surrey, B.C.: Heritage House Publishing Co. Ltd., 1993.

————. *Prince Ships of Northern B.C.* Surrey, B.C.: Heritage House Publishing Co. Ltd., 1995.

————. "B.C. Steamboat Days 1870-1883." *B.C. Historical Quarterly* 11, no. 2 (April 1947).

Hardy, W.G. *From Sea Unto Sea*. Toronto: Popular Library, 1960.

Harvey, R.G. *The Coast Connection*. Lantzville, B.C.: Oolichan Books, 1994.

Hoagland, Edward. *Notes from the Century Before: A Journal from British Columbia*. Toronto: Douglas & McIntyre, 1969.

Holmes, M.C. "Royal Commissions and Commissions of Enquiry in British Columbia: A Checklist. Part II: 1900-1910." *B.C. Historical Quarterly* 8, no. 4 (October 1944).

Hutchinson, Bruce. *The Fraser*. Rivers of America Books. New York/ Toronto: Rinehart and Co., 1950.

Johnston, Lukin. *Beyond the Rockies*. London: J.M. Dent & Sons Ltd., 1929.

Keith, Donald D. *Bush Pilot with a Briefcase*. Toronto: Doubleday Canada Ltd., 1972.

Kelly, William H. *The Mounties as They Saw Themselves*. Ottawa: The Golden Dog Press, 1996.

Kopas, Cliff. *Packhorses to the Pacific*. Sidney, B.C.: Gray's Publishing. Ltd., 1976.

Large, Dr. R.G. *The Skeena: River of Destiny*. Vancouver: Mitchell Press and Victoria: Gray's Publishing Ltd., 1957. Sixth edition published by Surrey, B.C.: Heritage House Publishing Co. Ltd., 1996.

Lee, Norman. *Klondike Cattle Drive*. Surrey, B.C.: Heritage House Publishing Company, Ltd., 1991.

Lindo, Millicent A., ed. *Making History*. Victoria: M.A. Lindo, publisher.

Lord, Alex. *Alex Lord's British Columbia*. Vancouver: UBC Press, 1992.

Mackay, Corday. "The Collins Overland Telegraph." *B.C. Historical Quarterly* 10, no. 3 (July 1946).

Morice, Rev. A.G. *History of the Northern Interior of British Columbia, formerly New Caledonia (1660 to 1880)*. Smithers, B.C.: Interior Stationery (1970) Ltd., 1970.

Neering, Rosemary. *Continental Dash*. Ganges, B.C.: Horsdal & Schubart Publishers Ltd., 1989.

Orchard, Imbert, ed. *Martin: The Story of a Young Fur Trader*. Sound Heritage No. 30. Aural History Program. Victoria: B.C. Archives & Records Service, 1981.

Ormsby, M.A. *British Columbia: A History*. Toronto: Macmillan, 1958.

Phillips, R.A.J. *Canada's Railways*. Canada at Work Series. Toronto: McGraw-Hill Company of Canada Limited, 1968.

Ramsey, Bruce. *Ghost Towns of British Columbia*. Vancouver: Mitchell Press Limited, 1963.

Richardson, Harold W. "Alcan: America's Glory Road." *Engineering News-Record*, December 17, 1942 and January 14, 1943.

Robinson, Noel. *Building An Historic Railway: The Memoirs of Henry J. Cambie*. New Westminster: News Advertiser Printers and Bookbinders.

Runnalls, Rev. F.E.. "Boom Days in Prince George." *B.C. Historical Quarterly* 8, no. 4 (October 1944).

Sage, Walter. "Record of a Trip to Dawson: The Diary of John Smith." *B.C. Historical Quarterly* 16 (January/April 1952).

Stumer, H. M. *This Was Klondike Fever*. Seattle: Superior Publishing Co., 1978.

Turner, Robert D. *The Pacific Princesses*. Victoria: Sono Nis Press, 1977.

———*Sternwheelers and Steam Tugs*. Victoria: Sono Nis Press, 1984.

Waite, Donald E. *The Langley Story*. Langley, B.C.: Don Waite Publishing, 1977.

Walker, Russell R.. *Bacon, Beans 'n Brave Hearts*. Lillooet, B.C.: Lillooet Publishers Ltd., 1972.

West, Willis J. *Stagecoach and Sternwheel Days in the Cariboo and Central B.C.* Surrey, B.C.: Heritage House Publishing Co. Ltd., 1985.

———. "The *B.X.* and the Rush to Fort George." *B.C. Historical Quarterly* 13, nos. 3 & 4 (July/October 1949).

Woodcock, George. *British Columbia: A History of the Province*. Vancouver: Douglas & McIntyre, 1990.

Young, Gerri F. *The Fort Nelson Story*. Fort Nelson, B.C.: Gerri F. Young, 1980.

VIDEO PRESENTATIONS

Ungar, George, director. *The Champagne Safari*. A 90-minute documentary on the life of Charles Bedaux, with footage from his expedition into the northern Rockies. 1995. Field Seven Films.

Waddington, Cal, with Steven G. Hites, Roy Minter, Larry Sullivan, and Marvin P. Taylor, all of the White Pass & Yukon Railway, Whitehorse, Yukon. *The Little Railway that Could*. Video presentation, 30 minutes. A. Logan Video Services Inc.

NEWSPAPERS & OTHER PUBLICATIONS

The British Colonist (New Westminster 1868, 1869)
The Cariboo Sentinel
The Engineering News-Record (December 17 and 31, 1942, January 14, 1943)
The Vancouver Province
The Vancouver Sun
The Victoria Times-Colonist

Index

Photo Credits

BCARS B-01269 (front cover), HP 61270 (p. 14), PDP 01348 (p. 19, t), PDP 01450 (p. 19, b), 22993 (p. 22), A-03049 (p. 23), A-03908 (p. 28), 69961 (p. 29, t), 10836 (p. 29, b), A-09678 (p. 30), 23040 (p. 32), HP 353 (p. 35), G-03259 (p. 36), No # (p.37, t, b), D-7686 (p. 38), C-8052 (p. 39, t), No # (p. 44, b), D-07320 (p. 47, t), B-03568 (p. 47, b), No # (p.55, t, b), 20388 (p. 56), C-05484 (p. 58), D-01382 (p. 59), D-01864 (p. 61), D-09561 (p. 62), B-01488 (p. 63, t), E-06563 (p. 63, m), A-02004 (p.63, b), A-03059 (p. 64), A-00433 (p. 67, t), D-05315 (p, 70), E-04102 (p. 72, 5), A-0962 (p. 72, b), 84201 (p. 74), E-05113 (p. 81), I-28239 (p. 83), A-00807 (p. 93), D-00890 (p. 98), D-03575 (p. 99), D-00369 (p. 101), I-33250 (p. 103), I-33249 (p. 104), I-33251 (p. 105), B-04444 (p. 106), B-05435 (p. 117, cover, r), B-05437 (p. 118), H-06875 (p. 121, t), D-00837 (p. 121,b), B-05438 (p. 123, t), I-28781 (p. 123, b), I-22190 (p. 127), I-22154 (p. 133), C-03766 (p. 136), G-07382 (p. 138), A-09127 (p. 139), 33791 (p. 140), G-08302 (p. 142), B-06922 (p. 143, l), B-06923 (p. 143, r), C-8567 (p. 145), F-09265 (p. 152), 13251 (p. 152), 721 (p. 154), A-5003 (p. 157, t), E-07590 (p. 162); E. White Collection (p. 33, t, 44, t); R.G. Harvey (p. 76, 79); Heritage House Collection (p. 33, m; 34, t, b; 40, 67, b; 100, 109), 139, t; 157, b); B.C. Provincial Museum PN 280 (back cover, l); Ministry of Public Works (p. 164); Ministry of Transportation and Highways (p. 87); Public Archives of Canada 21438 (p. 27), C-46169 (p. 39, b); Synod. Of the Diocese of New Caledonia, Prince Rupert (p. 65); University of Washington (p. 153); Vancouver Public Library 13556 (p. 33, b); Wrathall Collection (p. 60, 77).

Carving the Western Path: By River, Rail, and Road, Through B.C.'s Southern Mountains, is the companion volume to this book. It is also published by Heritage House. ISBN 1-895811-62-7

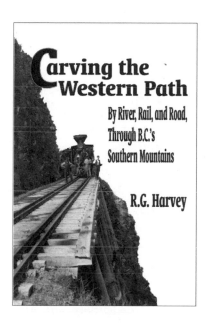

A century of deal making and government misdeeds form the backdrop for this entertaining account of sternwheelers, iron horses, and mountain roads. Battling factions of railbuilders carve up both the land the spoils of industry, throwing obstacles in the way of roads and ships alike. Discover why Kicking Horse Pass should never have been used as a rail route by the CPR and why the Kettle Valley Railway was a strategic mistake. Decide for yourself if railwaymen William Cornelius Van Horne and J.J. Hill were geniuses or opportunists. And meet real heroes who turned pathways into highways in spite of both political and natural adversity.

The Author

Bob Harvey joined the Department of Public Works of British Columbia in May of 1948, right in the middle of the worst spring flooding in 54 years. After some years as District Engineer at Nelson, then a few as the same at Nanaimo, he became Regional Maintenance Engineer at New Westminster, responsible for all provincial roads in Skeena, Prince Rupert, and Atlin districts, as well as Vancouver Island and the Lower Mainland. In 1958 he became Regional Highway Engineer at Prince George and took the northern districts with him to become responsible for all provincial roads north of Williams Lake, in what was by then the Ministry of Highways. He moved to Victoria in 1967 and became Deputy Minister of Highways and Public Works in 1976. He retired in 1983.